The MODERN FOOD PROCESSOR

RECIPE BOOK

101 Easy Family Meals You Can Make At Home

By Tara Adams

healthy happy Foodie

HHF Press

San Francisco

BON APPÉTIT!

CONTENTS

CHAPTER

1

WHY YOU NEED THIS BOOK

PRO TIPS ON HOW TO USE YOUR FOOD PROCESSOR

Tips to help save you time, get better results and avoid mistakes.
They have all been tested by experts to make sure they work.

UNLEASH THE FULL POTENTIAL OF YOUR FOOD PROCESSER

You probably don't realize the capabilities of your food processor, but it's capable of a lot. You'll learn how to make hash browns from scratch, soups, dips, and so much more using your food processor! This book will show you food you never thought about making with your food processor. You'll find that your food processor has endless possibilities.

THIS COOKBOOK WILL UNLOCK THE POTENTIAL OF YOUR FOOD PROCESSOR

This book will teach you all about your food processor and help you get the most out of it. A food processor makes so many kitchen tasks a breeze... Why not learn the pro tips, unofficial tricks, and recipes that will make it easier to enjoy better food?

101 OF THE MOST DELICIOUS RECIPES

This comprehensive book covers recipes for every meal. These 101 recipes are enough to last for months, and if you like to experiment in the kitchen, you can find endless variations for these recipes.

These recipes were created to maximize the unique capabilities of your food processor. They have been taste tested to make sure they meet the highest standards.

CHAPTER

2

THE BENEFITS OF A QUALITY FOOD PROCESSOR

COMPACT YET POWERFUL

Food processors are invaluable kitchen appliances because they allow you to process so many different types of food because they are small yet powerful. Best of all, a food processor takes up very little space in your kitchen and is easy to grab whenever it's needed.

STAINLESS STEEL BLADES FOR PERFECT CUTTING

Your food processor is equipped with stainless steel blades. Stainless steel is a very strong metal. These strong blades are incredibly sharp too. They'll stand up to all of your food challenges. They'll slice fruits with ease, and puree vegetable with no problem at all. These blades were made to last a long time too. You will get years of life out of them.

POWERFUL MOTOR TO KEEP YOUR FOOD PROCESSER GOING LONGER

Most quality food processors come equipped with a 450-watt motor. 450 watts is more power than a food processor needs. but manufacturers want to make sure their food processor can power through the toughest jobs. This extra power also ensures that your motor will last as long as your food processor does.

LARGE FEED TUBE TO CUT DOWN ON PREP TIME

Everybody hates taking extra time prepping food. Your food processor is equipped with a large feed to cut down on prep time. Smaller feed tubes force you to cut most vegetables into smaller pieces before you place them in your food processor. More cutting equals more prep time, but the large feed tube allows you to use bigger pieces, and even whole vegetables without a problem.

CHAPTER 3

WHY USE A FOOD PROCESSOR?

MAKE MEALS FASTER

Your food processor will allow you to make meals at lightning speed. Cutting vegetables by hand can be time consuming, but your food processor can do it in seconds. Grating potatoes for hash browns will take forever, but now you can let the food processor do all the work, and fast. Your food processor makes uniform cuts that would take forever by hand. Your food processor takes prep time down to its minimum so that you can focus on other things.

GIVE YOUR HANDS A BREAK

As I've mentioned your food processor, can do a lot of your chopping, and cutting needs. This takes so much strain off your hands. Those minutes of chopping, cutting, and mixing add up over time. They can contribute to sore muscles, and even arthritis. They can also make preexisting arthritis flare up. Let your food processor do the prepping for you, and give your hands a much needed rest.

MULTIPLE APPLIANCES IN ONE

A food processor is like have a bunch of small appliances in one. Puree fruits and vegetables like you would in a blender. Thinly slice vegetables like you would on a mandolin faster, and without the danger. Mix dressings and sauces without having to use a whisk. Grate vegetables without have to spend a long time using a peeler. No matter what you need to do your food processor can help you get it done easier and faster.

MAKE HEALTHY MEALS AT HOME INSTEAD OF GOING OUT

Many people choose to go out to eat instead of making meals, because of the time it takes to prepare food. Your food processor helps you cut down on prep time so that you can enjoy your meals faster. Making meals allows you to control what goes into your food. You can use healthier organic ingredients, avoid preservatives, harmful chemicals, and use healthier oils. You never know what's in food from a restaurant, but now you can in the comfort of your own home. Make wholesome healthy meals, instead of going out to eat fast food. You will feel better, and save money in the end.

CHAPTER

4

WHAT CAN YOUR FOOD PROCESSOR DO?

MAKE HOMEMADE NUT BUTTER

Store bought nut butter can be expensive, contain preservatives and harmful chemicals. On top of that some brands add sugar and excess salt. Your food processor can make nut butter in a few minutes. The best part is you get to control what goes into to it. You can get the exact consistency you want whether it's extra crunchy, or smooth. Make organic nut butter at a fraction of the cost of what you pay in the store.

GRIND YOUR OWN MEAT

Let's face it when you buy ground meat from the store you never know what's in it. Any part of the animal may be used, which includes parts with you might not want to eat. You can buy any cut of meat you like and make ground meat out of it. Simply put the meat in your food processor, and put the machine on speed 1. You'll have freshly ground meat in no time at all! Make sure you don't use frozen meat, because it can damage your machine.

CUT BUTTER INTO FLOUR

Making pie crust by hand can be time consuming. After mixing ingredients you have to cut in the butter, and who has time for that. Simply put the flour, cold butter, and salt for your pie crust in your food processor, and pulse it until it forms a meal. It should be around 10 seconds. Then add ice water a tablespoon at a time pulsing until the dough comes together. Put the dough on a floured surface, and form a ball. Flatten the ball into a disc. Cover and refrigerate for at least an hour.

MAKE HOMEMADE ICE CREAM

You may have thought that ice cream was something you bought at the store, or required an expensive ice cream maker. You can make delicious ice cream in your food processor. Now you can make ice cream in the comfort of your own home, and have a tasty treat for your kids. We have a great recipe for you in the recipe section.

MAKE HOMEMADE BUTTER

I'm sure many of you made butter as a kid in school. Either you used an old fashion churn or shook a jar until your small arms were ready to fall off. Imagine making this delicious treat at home without all the hassle of churning it by hand. You can make organic butter at home that tastes heavenly, and you can do it quickly. Imagine having fresh creamy butter whenever you want it without any preservatives. We have a recipe for it coming up later in the recipe section.

MAKE HOMEMADE POTATO CHIPS

Your food processor allows you to easily make potato chips at home. Making chips at home allows to control the entire process. You can make any flavor you want, use organic potatoes, and even choose what kind of oil you fry them in. All you have to do is use the slicing side of the disc. The potatoes will be sliced perfectly for chips. Fry them up, and add your favorite seasonings. You can also make delicious veggie chips.

CHAPTER
5

HOW TO USE YOUR FOOD PROCESSOR LIKE A PRO

NEVER BE AFRAID TO PAUSE

There is no food processor rule that says that you can't stop in the middle of your chop. Pause every once in a while to scrape foods off of the edges and make sure that the blades are moving freely. This will not only ensure the perfect consistency to your foods, but it will also extend the life of your blades and your machine. Be sure that the machine is completely turned off—you may even want to unplug the machine—before you check the blade for movement. When you are scraping the sides use a wooden spoon or rubber spatula to keep from scratching the bowl.

USING THE TUBE TO ITS MAXIMUM POTENTIAL

To really use the tube to its maximum potential, it starts at the blade. Always make sure that the blade is secure and tight so it doesn't wobble while you are feeding foods through the tube. This can ruin the blade and maybe even the machine if foods get lodged under the blade.

One of the many amazing features of your food processor is the tube, which is large enough to fit a whole block of cheese; to take advantage of this and make your own shredded cheese, start by placing the cheese in the tube and pressing it down with the plunger. Turn on the blade and continue to press the cheese block down with steady pressure until it is completely shredded.

For softer or partially frozen foods, you can employ the same type of procedure. Pack the food into the tub so there is little to no movement between foods in the tray. Press down with the plunger and turn the machine on, maintain even pressure until all ingredients have made it through the blade. With some smaller items like carrots, you can actually stack them together in the tube tightly which is nice because they end up being cut in perfectly even slices.

Perhaps the best way to make the most out of the tube is knowing how to use it to best prepare hard foods like nuts or hard cheeses. First, you want to break down the foods into portions that are small enough to fall through the tube without getting caught on the sides. Next, you want to make sure that the machine is already on and the blades are spinning—this is different than when you are cutting softer foods—finally, you want to drop pieces of the food in slowly this will allow the blades to do their job and will prevent hard foods from lodging underneath the blades.

USE A FUNNEL TO ADD LIQUIDS OR POWDERS

One of the worst parts about cooking is the clean up afterwards. It seems as though no matter what you do the entire counter is a mess after creating a decent meal; especially with a food processor. Food processors can be used to make all sorts of things including dough which uses both flour and water and can make a giant mess if spill in or around your processor. To cut down on the mess, get a kitchen funnel to help pour loose ingredients. By pouring the food through a funnel and straight into the processor tube you will save yourself the hassle of clean up and feel pretty smart while doing it.

HOW TO CLEAN AND STORE YOUR FOOD PROCESSOR

When it comes time to clean your processor always unplug it first. Take apart the machine so that all parts are separate. Almost every part is dishwasher safe so you can transfer each part to the dishwasher or to warm soapy water to be washed by hand. No matter how

you choose to wash the parts, execute extreme caution when washing the blades. They are incredibly sharp and with easily cut through a sponge and your hands if you are not careful. Wipe down the base with damp towel including around the dials and even the cord if you need to.

One of the great things about food processors is how easy they are to store because they're so compact.. Put the slicing blade on the motor shaft then turn the top upside down so the tube is inside the base. Place the plunger in the tube, then top with the shredding blade sharp side down to prevent injury. Once it is all together this machine is more compact than most countertop appliances.

HOW TO SHARPEN YOUR BLADES

Just like a kitchen knife dulls after prolonged use, the blades of your processor can dull as well. Doing this is not extremely difficult but it does take a few steps and you will need a sharpening stone. Hold the food processor blade by the plastic parts taking extra caution to keep your fingers away from the blades, even

if they are dull they could still do some damage to your fingers. Hold the sharpening stone with your fingers curled underneath and your thumb on top to ensure control of the blade.

Place the top edge of the sharpening stone over the edge of the blade and push it away from you across the blade. Press firmly, but not too hard and repeat the movement 4 or 5 times. Turn the blade over and repeat the same instructions, but move the stone toward you instead of away from you this time. Rinse the blade with cold water and allow to air dry.

3 SPEEDS FOR ALL OF YOUR NEEDS

Your food processor is equipped with 2 to 3 speeds to give you total control. The different speeds are great for different tasks. They ensure that you will great results every time no matter what you're doing.

PULSE

The pulse function gives you total control over how long the machine runs. The machine will only stay on as long as you hold the knob on pulse. It's great when you need a controlled chop, or if you are worried about over mixing something. It's perfect for getting your salsa to the right chunkiness.

SPEED 1

Speed 1 is great when you want to a rough chop, or are mixing things that won't get over mixed. If you're chopping up vegetables for a chunky soup, or using the disc to great vegetable and cheese this is the speed you want to use.

SPEED 2

Speed 2 is the fasted speed available on your food processor. This is the speed you want to use if you're pureeing fruits and vegetables. It's great for finely mincing sauces, and sauces like pesto. It's also the speed you want to use to make dips like hummus, and nut butters.

A DISC OR BLADE FOR ALL YOUR FOOD PROCESSING NEEDS

Your food processor comes with both a disk and blade to tackle every task. The blade chops, dices, minces, purees, and mixes. You'll want to use this to make nut butters, make pie crust dough, make butter, and most other things. You will also want to use the blade if you're grating hard cheese like parmesan. The blade will probably be the tool you use the most.

The disc has two sides for very specific purposes. One side is for grating. This is the side you want to use if you're grating cheese, or vegetables like potatoes, and carrots. The slicing side is what you'll use to get evenly sliced vegetables. This side is great for thinly sliced vegetables, great for salads, and making chips.

Whatever the task, you find that you'll be able to get it done with one of these two tools.

CLEANING YOUR FOOD PROCESSOR

Cleaning your food processer is simple. Place the bowl, lid, disc, blade, and food pusher in the top shelf of your dishwasher. Use a damp cloth or sponge to wipe off the base. If the base is very dirty, use a mild non-abrasive cleaner on it.

If you don't have a dishwasher, wash the bowl, lid, disc, blade, and food pusher in hot soapy water. Make sure to be very carefully when cleaning the disc, and blade. Dry all pieces with a towel, or let them dry on a drying rack.

STORING YOUR FOOD PROCESSOR

Since you will have so many uses for your food processor, it's a good idea to keep it on the counter where you will have easy access to it. Its compact sleek design makes it easy to keep on the counter. You can easily store all the parts in your food processor. Simply place the chopping blade on the motor shaft. Then put the lid on top of the bowl upside down. Then put the food pusher into the food shoot. Finally place the disk on top of the lid. Now you can store all the parts in one place, and avoid losing any piece.

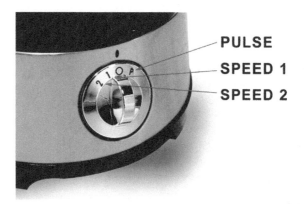

PULSE
SPEED 1
SPEED 2

CHAPTER

6

PRO TIPS

USE CHILLED CHEESE WHEN SHREDDING

Cheese can fall apart when you're shredding it if it's not hard enough. Place your semi-firm cheese in the refrigerator for a little while to firm it up. You will get a much better shred if you do. Avoid shredding a soft cheese like buffalo mozzarella in your food processor. They're too soft to shred and will only make a mess in your food processor

STAY AWAY FROM PUREEING AND MASHING STARCHY VEGETABLES

Starchy vegetables like potatoes, and some types of squash shouldn't be pureeing in a food processor. The spinning of the food processor sets off the starch. The starch will create a glue like sticky mixture in your food processor that's no fun to clean up, and doesn't make for delicious food.

DON'T OVERFILL THE BOWL WITH LIQUID

Never fill your food processor more than a quarter of the way full of liquid. When the food processor is on it will agitate the liquid and it will fly all over the place before leaking out of the sides. If you have a large amount of liquid ingredients, processes them in batches instead of all at once. It will save you a lot of clean up time.

PULSE YOUR FOODS FOR THE RIGHT LENGTH OF TIME

Pulsing for the right amount of time is important if you want the perfect chop. If you don't do it long enough, the chop is too coarse. If you do it too long, the ingredients start turning into liquid. The ideal pulse is 1 second at a time. It just enough time to chop ingredients without turning them into liquid. Pulse for 1 second at a time until the desired consistency is reached.

HOW TO GET ALL OF YOUR WET INGREDIENTS OUT OF YOUR FOOD PROCESSOR

After you've made a sauce like pesto or a nut butter, there's residue left on the blades, and bottom of the base. All you need to do is put the lid back on, and turn the food processor back on for a second or two. The remaining liquid will fly onto the sides of the bowl. Here you can use a spatula to scrape the liquid off the sides, and use them. It also makes for a cleaner machine and cuts down on clean up time.

CHAPTER
7

SOUPS

BROCCOLI SOUP

Servings: 5 | Prep Time: 10 Minutes | Cook Time: 40 Minutes

INGREDIENTS

5 cups chicken stock

1 pound broccoli, chopped

1 medium onion, chopped

1 garlic clove, minced

Black pepper to taste

1 tablespoon lemon juice

2 tablespoons curry powder, to taste (optional)

This is a healthy take on traditional broccoli soup. This recipe replaces cream with chicken stock, which is much healthier.

DIRECTIONS

1. Chop the garlic, and onion. Mince the garlic.

2. In a large pot, bring the chicken stock to a boil on medium heat. Once boiling, put in the onions, garlic, and broccoli. Allow the mixture to simmer for around 30 minutes, until the vegetable are soft.

3. Once the vegetables are soft, allow the soup to cool a little, and then put it in your food processor. Puree the soup on speed 2 in batches. Then put the soup back in the pot

4. Add in the pepper, lemon juice, and the curry powder (if desired), and mix well.

5. Serve hot soup in bowls.

Nutritional Info: Calories: 59 | Sodium: 797mg | Dietary Fiber: 3.7g | Total Fat: 1.2g | Total Carbs: 10.5g | Protein: 3.8g.

BUFFALO CHICKEN SOUP

Servings: 6 | Prep Time: 15 Minutes | Cook Time: 30 Minutes

INGREDIENTS

2 pounds rotisserie chicken, cooked

3 tablespoons ranch seasoning

1 large head cauliflower

4 cups chicken stock

2 cups chicken broth

1 cup water

1 pound carrots

6 stalks celery

1 medium onion

1 tablespoon butter

1 cup hot sauce

Chopped green onion and blue cheese crumbles for garnish

This soup is nice and creamy with a smooth texture. It gets a nice kick from the buffalo sauce, and makes a great dish for football games.

DIRECTIONS

1. Shred the chicken. Dice the onions and celery. Slice the carrots and chop the cauliflower.

2. Place the cauliflower, chicken broth, chicken stock, ranch seasoning, and water in a stock pot and bring to a boil. Boil for about 10 minutes until the cauliflower becomes tender. Then allow the mixture to cool down a bit.

3. While the mixture is cooling, put the butter in a sauté pan and melt it on medium heat. Add in the celery, onion, and carrots. Allow the vegetable to cook until the onions are translucent, and soft.

4. Place the cooled mixture in your food processor in batches, and puree it on speed 2. Transfer it back to the pot.

5. Put the hot sauce in, and mix well.

6. Add the sautéed vegetables to the pot, and mix.

7. Mix in the chicken, and let the soup cook on low heat for around 20 to 30 minutes. Serve with a garnish of green onion, and crumbled blue cheese.

Nutritional Info: Calories: 321 | Sodium: 2474mg | Dietary Fiber: 8.3g | Total Fat: 4.2g | Total Carbs: 26.3g | Protein: 44.5g.

BUTTERNUT SQUASH AND LEEK SOUP

> Servings: 8 | Prep Time: 15 Minutes | Cook Time: 1 Hour 5 Minutes

INGREDIENTS

4-1/2 pounds butternut squash

5 tablespoons unsalted butter

4 large leeks

7 fresh thyme sprigs or 1 teaspoon dried

5 cups chicken stock

1-1/4 teaspoons salt

1/2 teaspoon freshly ground pepper

1/2 cup sour cream

3 tablespoons chopped chives

8 slices of bacon

This soup has beautiful orange color because of the butternut squash. It's nice and light, and makes a good starter to a winter meal.

DIRECTIONS

1. Preheat your oven to 350F. Halve the butternut squash lengthwise. Coarsely chop the white and soft green parts of the leeks. Chop the chives.

2. On a baking sheet, put on the squash with the cut side down. Put it in the oven, and bake for around 40 minutes. The squash should be tender. Allow it to cool a bit and then scoop out the flesh.

3. While the squash is baking, melt the butter on low heat in a large saucepan. Once the butter is melted, add the thyme and leeks, and cook until the leeks have browned, and are soft. Then remove the thyme leaves.

4. Add in the squash and stalk. Raise to medium heat, and let the mixture simmer for 20 minutes.

5. Once cooked, place the soup in your food processor, and puree in batches on speed 2 until smooth. Then transfer the soup back to the pan, and salt and pepper to taste.

6. Garnish with pieces of bacon, chives, and sour cream.

Nutritional Info: Calories: 402 | Sodium: 1569mg | Dietary Fiber: 6.2g | Total Fat: 22.7g | Total Carbs: 39.5g | Protein: 14.8g.

CARROT CARDAMOM SOUP

Servings: 4-6 | Prep Time: 15 Minutes | Cook Time: 1 Hour 5 Minutes

INGREDIENTS

2 tablespoons olive oil

1 medium white onion

3 tablespoons fresh ginger

1 tablespoon cardamom spice blend

5 large carrots

1 red bell pepper

1 medium Idaho potato

1 medium sweet potato

8 cups chicken stock

2 cups dry white wine

1 tablespoon light brown sugar

1/2 cup fresh lime juice

1/2 cup fresh Italian (flat-leaf) parsley

1/2 stick unsalted butter

Salt and freshly ground black pepper, to taste

Lime slices, for garnish

The spices in this soup take it to the next level. The cardamom transforms this basic carrot soup to an aromatic, flavorful sensation.

DIRECTIONS

1. Peel and cut the potato, and sweet potato into 1/2-inch pieces. Peel and cut the carrots into 1/4-nch pieces. Stem, seed, and cut the bell pepper into 1/4-inch pieces. Chop the parsley and onion. Peel and chop the ginger. Cut the butter into pieces

2. In a large stock pot, heat the oil on medium heat. Mix in red bell pepper, potatoes, spice blend, ginger, carrots, red pepper, and onion. Make sure the vegetables are completely coated in oil.

3. Let them cook for 15 minutes, until the onions are tender, and translucent.

4. Put in the brown sugar, wine, and chicken stock. Let the mixture boil, then lower the heat, and let the mixture simmer for 30-40 minutes, covered, until the vegetables are soft. Let the soup cool for a little bit.

5. Put the soup in your food processor in batches, and puree on speed 2, until smooth. Transfer the soup back to the pot.

6. Add in the parsley and lime juice, stir well, then put in the butter, salt and pepper to taste. Let soup cook on low heat until the butter is completely melted, and mixed into the soup.

7. Serve and garnish with lime slices if desired.

Nutritional Info: Calories: 294 | Sodium: 1133mg | Dietary Fiber: 4.6g | Total Fat: 13.5g | Total Carbs: 28.1g | Protein: 3.6g.

CAULIFLOWER SOUP

Servings: 6 | Prep Time: 15 Minutes | Cook Time: 45 Minutes

INGREDIENTS

3 tablespoons butter

4 large shallots

7-8 garlic cloves

1/2 cup celery

2 heads cauliflower

32-ounce chicken stock

1 tablespoon fresh thyme

1/2 teaspoon pepper

1 teaspoon salt

1/4 teaspoon red pepper flake

1 cup parmesan cheese

3 tablespoons corn starch + 3 tablespoons water

1 lemon, juice

This soup is delightfully creamy, but low in calories. It is packed with flavor, but has a delicate taste.

DIRECTIONS

1. Chop the shallots, garlic, celery, and thyme. Roughly chop the cauliflower.

2. In a large pot, brown the butter on medium heat, this should take 3-5 minutes. Increase the heat to medium-high and put in the garlic, celery, and shallots.

3. Cook for 5-7 minutes until the veggies brown a little, and soften. Once softened, put in the chicken stock, cauliflower, pepper, and salt.

4. Cover the mixture, and allow it to come to a simmer. Let the mixture simmer for 15-20 minutes, the cauliflower should be tender.

5. Once tender, put the soup in your food processor. Let the soup cool a little, and then puree it on speed 2, until it's smooth. Transfer the soup back to the pot.

6. Whisk together the corn starch and water. Add that, the red pepper flakes, and parmesan cheese to the soup.

7. Allow the soup to simmer again for 5-10 minutes, and let it thicken. Mix in the lemon juice, and more salt if necessary.

8. Serve soup hot.

Nutritional Info: Calories: 249 | Sodium: 1377mg | Dietary Fiber: 2.7g | Total Fat: 14.8g | Total Carbs: 16.9g | Protein: 15.7g.

CREAMY ASPARAGUS SOUP

Servings: 6 cups | Prep Time: 10 Minutes | Cook Time: 15 Minutes

INGREDIENTS

2 tablespoons butter (or olive oil if making this vegan/dairy-free/paleo)

1 onion

1 stalk of celery

1 clove of garlic

1 russet potato

3 cups asparagus

5 cups of chicken or vegetable stock

1/4 teaspoon ground black pepper

1 teaspoon lemon juice

1 cup asparagus tips only (optional for garnish)

You'll be amazed that this soup contains no dairy at all. Instead it uses potatoes to give it its thick and creamy textures. It's great on a rainy spring day.

DIRECTIONS

1. Chop the potato, onion, and celery. Mince the garlic. Cut the asparagus into 1 inch pieces and discard the woody ends.

2. Melt the butter on medium-high heat in a large pot. Once melted, add the celery, garlic, and onions.

3. Cook the vegetables until the onions are translucent. Once translucent, mix in the potato, and asparagus.

4. Pour in the stock, and let the mixture simmer.

5. Bring down the heat to low, and continue to simmer until the vegetable are soft, around 15 minutes

6. Let the soup cool a little bit, and then process it in your food processor in batches, on speed 2, until smooth.

7. Transfer the soup back to the pot, and place it on low heat. Add in the lemon juice and pepper, stirring occasionally. Cook for a couple minutes until flavors combine, and the soup is hot.

8. Garnish with asparagus tips, and serve with crackers if desired.

Nutritional Info: Calories: 91 | Sodium: 670mg | Dietary Fiber: 3.0g | Total Fat: 4.5g | Total Carbs: 11.1g | Protein: 3.4g.

POTATO BACON AND LEEK SOUP

Servings: 4-6 | Prep Time: 30 Minutes | Cook Time: 30 Minutes

INGREDIENTS

25g butter

3 slices of fatty bacon

1 onion

400g packed leek

3 medium potatoes

1-1/2 quarts vegetable stock

142ml cream

4 slices fatty bacon

DIRECTIONS

1. Chop the onion, and peel and dice the potatoes. Trim the leek, wash it thoroughly, and slice it.

2. In a large pan, melt the butter on medium heat. Once melted, add in the bacon and onions. Stir often until the onions brown.

3. Then add the potatoes and leeks. Mix well, then cover the pan, and lower the heat.

4. Allow the mixture to cook for 5 minutes, shaking the pan occasionally to make sure the ingredients don't stick to the pan.

5. After 5 minutes, add the stock, and bring to a boil. Then lower heat and let soup simmer, cover for about 20 minutes. The vegetables should be soft.

6. Allow the soup to cool for a little before, putting it in your food processor. Then process the soup in batches on speed 2 until it's nice and smooth.

7. Then put it back in the pan, and add the cream. Heat the soup on low heat until it's warm enough to serve, and salt and pepper to taste.

8. Serve in bowls, with a garnish of crispy bacon.

Nutritional Info: Calories: 199 | Sodium: 912mg | Dietary Fiber: 4.2g | Total Fat: 7.3g | Total Carbs: 29.3g | Protein: 5.6g.

ROASTED PUMPKIN SOUP

Servings: 5 | Prep Time: 5 Minutes | Cook Time: 60 Minutes

INGREDIENTS

1 small pumpkin

2 tablespoons coconut oil, divided

1 medium yellow onion, chopped

2 medium parsnips, chopped

2 medium carrots, chopped

3 garlic cloves, chopped

1 tablespoon chopped fresh ginger

1 teaspoon dried thyme

1/2 teaspoon dried sage

1/2 teaspoon pumpkin pie spice

1/4 teaspoon chili powder

3 cups vegetable or chicken stock

Sea salt to taste

This soup has a savory taste thanks to the roasting and spices. It's a perfect soup for the fall and winter months.

DIRECTIONS

1. Preheat the oven to 350F.

2. Slice the pumpkin in half. Then remove the stem and seeds. Grease a baking sheet, and put the pumpkin on it sliced side down. Place the pumpkin on the oven for about 35 minutes, until the pumpkin is tender.

3. Let the pumpkin cool and then scoop out the flesh. Throw away the skin.

4. While the pumpkin is cooling, heat the remaining coconut oil on medium heat in a large pot. Once heated put in the parsnips, garlic, ginger, carrots, and onions.

5. Sauté the vegetables until the onions become translucent, and the other vegetables start to soften, about 10 minutes.

6. Then put in the stock, chili powder, pumpkin, sage, thyme, and pumpkin pie spice. Bring the soup to a boil then let it simmer, on lower heat, covered, until the vegetables are completely tender, around 15 minutes.

7. Put the soup in your food processor in batches. Let it cool for a bit, and then puree it on speed 2 until smooth.

8. Put the soup back in the pot warm it back up and salt to taste. Serve in bowls, and garnish with either herbs or roasted pumpkin seeds.

Nutritional Info: Calories: 237 | Sodium: 501mg | Dietary Fiber: 14.2g | Total Fat: 7.1g | Total Carbs: 44.1g | Protein: 5.6g.

SUMMER SQUASH CORN CHOWDER

Servings: 5 | Prep Time: 20 Minutes | Cook Time: 20 Minutes

INGREDIENTS

6 slices bacon, cooked and crumbled and 4 teaspoon rendered bacon fat reserved

1 cup green onions

1/2 cup celery

1-1/2 pounds yellow squash

2 cloves garlic

2-3/4 cups milk

4-1/2 cups corn kernel

1/2 cup heavy cream

1/2 teaspoon dried thyme

3/4 teaspoons salt

1/4 teaspoon freshly ground black pepper

3/4 cups shredded cheddar cheese

The squash and corn give this soup a light, sweet flavor. It's very refreshing on a warm summer night, and makes a great first course.

DIRECTIONS

1. Mince the garlic. Slice the celery thinly. Chop the squash. Slice the green onions.

2. Cook, and crumble the bacon. Save 4 tablespoons of the bacon fat.

3. In a large pot, heat the bacon fat on medium heat. Once heated, put in the celery squash, and 3/4 cups of green onion. Cook for about 8 minutes, during the last 30 seconds put in the garlic, and continue cooking. Lower the heat to medium.

4. Put thyme, salt and pepper, 1-1/2 cups of corn, and 1-1/2 cups of milk, in the pot.

5. Place the cream, remaining milk, and remaining corn into your food processor, and process on speed 1 until almost pureed. Transfer the mixture to the pot.

6. Mix all ingredients well, and heat until desired temperature is reached.

7. Serve with a garnish of cheese, and crumbled bacon.

Nutritional Info: Calories: 501 | Sodium: 1325mg | Dietary Fiber: 5.5g | Total Fat: 28.1g | Total Carbs: 40.9g | Protein: 27.1g.

TUSCAN WHITE BEAN SOUP

Servings: 6-8 | Prep Time: 15 Minutes | Cook Time: 20 Minutes

INGREDIENTS

2 tablespoons extra virgin olive oil

1 small yellow onion

2 stalks celery stalk

4 garlic cloves

2 teaspoons dried oregano

1 teaspoon dried thyme

1 teaspoon dried basil

1 teaspoon dried ground sage

2 carrots

2 tomatoes

5 cups vegetable stock

1 can cannellini beans

1 tablespoon sage

1 pinch salt and pepper, to taste

The Italian cannellini beans give this vegetable soup a wonderful texture. The spices give a world of flavor to this healthy soup.

DIRECTIONS

1. Finely chop the yellow onion, and dice the celery stalks and carrots. Mince the garlic, and finely chop the sage. Drain and rinse the cannellini beans. Chop and seed the tomatoes.

2. Using a large pot, heat the olive oil on medium-high heat. Once the oil is heated, put in the garlic, onions, and celery. Cook until the onions are translucent, around 3 minutes.

3. Once translucent, pit in the oregano, carrots, tomatoes, carrots, basil, sage, and time. Stir occasionally, and let the mixture cook for around 5 minutes.

4. After the 5 minutes put in the cannellini beans, and vegetable stock. Allow the soup to simmer. Once simmering, let the soup simmer for 10 minutes. Stir occasionally.

5. Put 1/2 the soup, or a little less in your food processor.

6. Let the soup cool a little and then turn the machine to speed 1 until the soup is creamy.

7. Transfer it back to the pot with the rest of the soup, and mix well. Once mixed salt and pepper to taste.

8. Serve soup in bowls, and garnish with sage.

Nutritional Info: Calories: 134 | Sodium: 499mg | Dietary Fiber: 7.1g | Total Fat: 4.2g | Total Carbs: 18.9g | Protein: 6.6g.

CHAPTER
8
APPETIZERS

ANCHOVY ONION GALETTE

Servings: 12 | Prep Time: at least 90 Minutes | Cook Time: 1 Hour 20 Minutes

INGREDIENTS

FOR PASTRY:

1-1/4 cups all-purpose flour

1 stick unsalted butter

1/4 teaspoon salt

3 - 5 tablespoons ice water

FOR FILLING:

2 large onions

2 tablespoons olive oil

2 tablespoons unsalted butter

5 - 6 anchovy fillets

1 garlic clove

2 tablespoons tomato paste

1/2 teaspoon dried thyme

This is a twist on a French provincial dish. It gets a beautiful complement of flavors from the caramelized onions, anchovies, and tomato paste. It can also work as a lunch when paired with a salad.

Nutritional Info: Calories: 189 | Sodium: 198mg | Dietary Fiber: 2.1g | Total Fat: 12.3g | Total Carbs: 17.6g | Protein: 3.0g.

DIRECTIONS

FOR PASTRY:

1. Cut the butter into 1/2-inch cubes.

2. Put the flour, butter, and salt in your food processor, and pulse until it becomes a meal, with small lumps of butter still in it.

3. Spread 3 tablespoons of water over the mixture, and pulse until well mixed. Check the dough by squeezing a small amount, and seeing if it holds together.

4. Add 1/2 tablespoon water and pulse again if it doesn't. Repeat the process until the dough passes the test.

5. Put the mixture on a lightly floured surface, and separate it into 4 equal pieces. Press each piece down using a forward motion with the heel of your hand a couple of times.

6. Create a ball out of the 4 pieces, and flatten it into a 5-inch disk. Wrap it in plastic wrap, and place it in the refrigerator for at least an hour.

7. For the caramelized onion, while the dough is chilling, slice the onions. Heat the oil and butter in a large skillet on medium heat, and add in the onions. Cook the onions for 30 minutes, until they soften, and turn golden, stirring occasionally.

8. Making the Galette:

9. Preheat your oven to 350F. Crumble the thyme. Finely chop the garlic and anchovies, and mix together.

10. Combine the anchovy and garlic mixture with the tomato paste, and thyme.

11. Place the chilled dough on a lightly floured surface, and roll it out into a 13-inch circle using a rolling pin. Then put it on a baking sheet lined with parchment paper.

12. Cover the dough with anchovy mixture, keeping a 2-inch dough border. Then put the onions on top of the anchovy mixture. Carefully fold the dough edges inward. Bake for 45 to 50 minutes, until he pastry is golden brown.

13. The galette can be served at room temperature or warm.

CAULIFLOWER TOTS

Servings: 35 Tots | Prep Time: 30 Minutes | Bake Time: 45 Minutes

INGREDIENTS

2 medium heads cauliflower

1/4 cup small onion

1/4 cup grated parmesan cheese

1/4 cup finely ground breadcrumbs

1 large egg

These are a healthier alternative to traditional potato based tater tots. They're an easy way to get kids to eat vegetables, and are baked instead of fried.

DIRECTIONS

1. Cut the cauliflower into florets. Dice the onions. Preheat your oven to 350F. Grease a nonstick baking sheet.

2. In a large pot, boil salted water. Once boiling, add the cauliflower, and cook for 5 to 10 minutes, until tender.

3. Place the cauliflower in your food processor, and pulse until the cauliflower resembles grains of rice. This should take a few seconds.

4. Put 3 cups of well packed cauliflower into a big bowl. Mix in the parmesan, egg, breadcrumbs, onion, and salt and pepper to taste.

5. Shape 1 to 2 tablespoon chunks of the mixture into tater tot form using your hands. Place the newly formed tater tots on the baking sheet. Space the tater tots 1 inch apart from each other.

6. Place the tots in the oven and let them bake for 20 minutes, and then turn them over. Let them bake on the other sides until they're crispy, about 10 to 15 minutes.

7. Serve hot with your favorite dipping sauce.

Nutritional Info: Calories: 22 | Sodium: 30mg | Dietary Fiber: 1.5g | Total Fat: 0.4g | Total Carbs: 3.8g | Protein: 1.6g.

CHEDDAR BACON CRACKERS

Servings: 54 Crackers | Prep Time: 10 Minutes | Bake Time: 15 Minutes

INGREDIENTS

2 cups flour

1 teaspoon baking powder

1/2 teaspoon cayenne pepper

1 cup butter

2 cups shredded cheddar cheese

1 cup cooked bacon pieces

1/4 cup milk

These crackers are filled with the delicious flavors of cheddar and bacon. The dough comes together quickly in your food processor.

DIRECTIONS

1. Cube the butter, and make sure it's cold. Chop the bacon. Use parchment paper to line a baking sheet. Preheat your oven to 375F.

2. Put the baking powder, flour, butter, and cayenne in your food processor, and pulse until the mixture forms a crumbly dough.

3. Then add in the milk, cheese, and bacon, and pulse again until a dough forms. Make sure not to over process it.

4. Scoop dough in 1 tablespoon balls onto the baking sheet. Then flatten the balls down using a floured fork.

5. Make crisscross patterns with the fork if desired. Bake the crackers for 12-15, until they brown.

Nutritional Info: Calories: 110 | Sodium: 245mg | Dietary Fiber: 0g | Total Fat: 8.4g | Total Carbs: 3.8g | Protein: 4.7g.

CRISPY CAULIFLOWER AND CHEESE BITES

Servings: 12 | Prep Time: 10 Minutes | Bake Time: 15 Minutes

INGREDIENTS

1/2 cauliflower head

125g grated cheddar

1 teaspoon freshly cracked black pepper

1 free range egg

These bite sized cakes make a great snack. They're a delicious way to sneak more vegetables into your kids' diet.

DIRECTIONS

1. Roughly chop the cauliflower. Preheat the oven to 400F. Lightly grease a muffin tin.

2. Put the cauliflower in your food processor, and pulse until the cauliflower resembles grains of rice. It should take a few seconds.

3. Mix all the ingredients in a large bowl until well combined.

4. Put 1-1/2 tablespoons of the mixture in each hole in the muffin tray. Bake for 15 minutes. Serve the bites hot.

Nutritional Info: Calories: 34 | Sodium: 82mg | Dietary Fiber: 1.1g | Total Fat: 1.1g | Total Carbs: 2.6g | Protein: 3.9g.

FINGERLING POTATO SALAD WITH CILANTRO JALAPENO SALSA

Servings: 8 | Prep Time: 10 Minutes | Cook Time: 15 Minutes

INGREDIENTS

4 pounds fingerling potatoes

4 tablespoons cider vinegar

3 fresh jalapeño chilies

2 cups fresh cilantro sprigs

1-1/2 shallots

1 garlic clove

1/4 cup extra-virgin olive oil

This is a complete departure from traditional potato salad that uses mayonnaise. This salad is slightly spicy with a southwestern flavor.

DIRECTIONS

1. Coarsely chop the shallot, garlic, and cilantro. Using gloves, remove the seeds and ribs from 2 of the jalapenos. Chop the jalapenos. Make sure you don't touch your eyes when handling jalapenos.

2. Place the potatoes in a large pot, and pour in enough cold water to cover the potatoes by an inch. Salt the water. Bring the water to a simmer, and let the potatoes simmer for 10 to 15 minutes, until they're tender.

3. While the potatoes are boiling, put the cilantro, shallots, garlic, olive oil, 3 tablespoons of vinegar, and jalapenos in your food processor. Pulse the ingredients until they're all finely chopped.

4. When the potatoes are done cooking, run them under cold water to help them cool. Cut them lengthwise.

5. Use the remaining vinegar to toss the potatoes while they're still somewhat warm. Salt and pepper to taste when the potatoes have reached room temperature.

6. Mix the potatoes with the salsa, until the potatoes are well covered.

7. Serve immediately.

Nutritional Info: Calories: 220 | Sodium: 16mg | Dietary Fiber: 4.1g | Total Fat: 6.7g | Total Carbs: 37.3g | Protein: 4.6g.

GRILLED VEGETABLE FLATBREAD WITH ZUCCHINI EGGPLANT AND TOMATO

Servings: 8 | Prep Time: 10 Minutes | Cook Time: 30 Minutes

INGREDIENTS

2 zucchini

2 eggplants

2 heirloom tomatoes

2 roasted red bell peppers

1 tablespoon extra-virgin olive oil

1/4 cup olive oil

1 onion

2 cups lima beans

1/4 cup grated Parmesan

1 tablespoon parsley

1 teaspoon lemon zest

1/4 teaspoon fresh thyme

1/4 cup vegetable or chicken broth

4 flatbreads or pitas, uncut

These flatbreads are a lovely Mediterranean starter. They're healthy too, providing 8 grams of fiber per serving.

DIRECTIONS

1. Cut the zucchini and eggplant into 1/3-inch slices. Cut the tomatoes into 1/4-inch slices. Cut the roasted red bell peppers into 2-inch slices. Chop the onions, and parsley.

2. Lightly coat the tomatoes, zucchini, and eggplant with the extra-virgin olive oil using a brush, and salt and pepper to taste. Grill them until they're tender.

3. Heat 2 tablespoons of olive oil in a pan on medium-low heat. Add in the onions and cook until they caramelize, stir occasionally, around 15 to 20 minutes.

4. Place the lima beans, Parmesan, onions, thyme, lemon zest, and parsley in your food processor, and puree it on speed 2. While the machine is pureeing add the stock, and 2 tablespoons of olive oil. Once smooth, salt and pepper to taste.

5. Toast the flatbread on both sides. Spread the pureed mixture on the warm flatbreads, and place the vegetables on the puree. Serve immediately.

Nutritional Info: Calories: 287 | Sodium: 319mg | Dietary Fiber: 8.9g | Total Fat: 13.8g | Total Carbs: 30.6g | Protein: 13.9g.

PEA FRITTERS

Servings: 12 | Prep Time: 5 Minutes | Cook Time: 9 Minutes

INGREDIENTS

3 cups frozen peas

3 eggs

11/4 cups self-rising flour

1 spring onion

1/3 cup crumbled feta cheese

2 tablespoons parsley

These delicious little cakes are a great way to get your kids to eat their vegetables. They taste great both hot and cold, so they make a good addition to a school lunch.

DIRECTIONS

1. Chop the onions and parsley.

2. Place the peas in a pot with water, and boil for 4 minutes.

3. Put half of the peas, flour, eggs, onion in your food processor and pulse until the ingredients are combined

4. Fold the feta, parsley, and remaining 1-1/2 cups of peas into the mixture.

5. Using a little oil, fry spoonful of the mixture. Fry the fritters for 2 minutes on each side.

Nutritional Info: Calories: 163 | Sodium: 92mg | Dietary Fiber: 3.0g | Total Fat: 2.4g | Total Carbs: 27.9g | Protein: 7.0g.

SHRIMP REMOULADE

Servings: 4 | Prep Time: At least 4 hours

INGREDIENTS

1/2 cup celery

1/3 cup green onion

1 tablespoon fresh tarragon

2 tablespoons dijon mustard

1 tablespoon horseradish

1 teaspoon capers

2 teaspoons paprika

1/4 - 1/2 teaspoon cayenne pepper

1 clove garlic

1/4 cup olive oil

fresh cracked pepper and kosher salt

1 pound prawns, cooked, peeled and chilled

Lettuce leaves

Shrimp remoulade is a traditional dish from New Orleans. This version has a nice mustardy flavor that gives it a tang. Make the sauce a day in advance and leave it to chill in the fridge for the best flavor.

DIRECTIONS

1. Chop the garlic and tarragon. Grate the horseradish. Dice the onion and celery.

2. Put the first 9 ingredients in your food processor, and puree them on speed 2 until they're smooth.

3. While the ingredients are being pureed pour the olive oil in slowly until the sauce comes together.

4. Salt and pepper to taste. Put the sauce in the refrigerator covered for at least 4 hours.

5. Place about 1/3 of the sauce in a bowl. Add the cold shrimp, and toss until the shrimp is covered.

6. Place the shrimp on the lettuces leave, and serve with a side of the sauce.

Nutritional Info: Calories: 284 | Sodium: 323mg | Dietary Fiber: 2.0g | Total Fat: 16.5g | Total Carbs: 6.9g | Protein: 27.9g.

STUFFED ZUCCHINI WITH PECORINO SAUCE

Servings: 6 | Prep Time: 20 Minutes | Bake Time: 1 Hour 40 Minutes

INGREDIENTS

12 zucchinis

2 tablespoons unsalted butter

2 tablespoons olive oil

2 large shallots

1 tablespoon parsley

1 tablespoon thyme

1/4 cup grated cheese

Salt and freshly ground pepper

2 eggs

PECORINO SAUCE:

2 hard-cooked large egg yolks

1/3 cup extra-virgin olive oil

2 1/2 cups finely grated young sheep's milk cheese

1/3 cup water, more if desired

Salt

These zucchinis are bursting with flavor thanks to the cheese, and herbs they're stuffed with. The pecorino gives it a lovely slightly salty flavor.

Nutritional Info: Calories: 482 | Sodium: 417mg | Dietary Fiber: 4.8g | Total Fat: 39.8g | Total Carbs: 16.5g | Protein: 20.9g.

DIRECTIONS

1. Finely chop the parsley, and shallots. Preheat your oven to 350F. Grease a large baking dish.

2. Slice 8 of the zucchini into 2-inch pieces crosswise. Hollow out the center of each zucchini leaving a 1/4-inch border, with a melon baller, do not discard the flesh. Mince the remaining 4 zucchinis and the scooped out flesh.

3. Melt the butter in the olive on medium heat in a large skillet. Put in the shallot and cook for around 3 minutes, until the shallots are translucent.

4. Put in the minced zucchini, stir occasionally, until the zucchini brown and become tender, around 25 minutes. Then mix in the thyme and parsley.

5. Put the zucchini in your processor and puree on speed 2 until smooth. Transfer the puree to a bowl, mix in the Parmigiano-Reggiano, and salt and pepper to taste.

6. Let the mixture cool. While the mixture is cooling, light beat the eggs. Once the mixture is cooled, mix in the eggs. Put the hollowed out zucchini in the baking dish with the hollow side up.

7. Stuff with the zucchini filling, making sure to mound it a little. Bake for an hour and 10 minutes.

8. Put the egg yolks and olive oil in your food processor and puree on speed 2 until the ingredients become a smooth paste. Put in 1/3 cup of water and the pecorino and puree on speed 2 again until the mixture becomes similar to heavy cream. If the sauce is too think add more water. Salt to taste.

9. Cover a plate with the sauce, and place the baked zucchini on top of it.

SNAILS IN GARLIC HERB BUTTER

Servings: 2 | Prep Time: 10 Minutes | Cook Time: 10 Minutes

INGREDIENTS

5 ounces escargots snails, rinsed

4 tablespoons unsalted butter, softened

1-1/2 teaspoons garlic, minced

2 tablespoons fresh flat-leaf parsley, finely chopped

1 tablespoon shallots, minced

Sea salt

Ground black pepper

10 each snail shells

This dish isn't for everybody, but those that are willing to try it are rewarded by the woodsy flavor of the snails, and their tender texture. The sauce gives it a beautiful garlic taste

DIRECTIONS

1. Rinse the snail. Set the butter out to soften. Mince the garlic and shallots. Finely chop the parsley. Preheat your oven to 400F.

2. Place the shallots, garlic, butter, and parsley in your food processor, and puree it on speed 2 until smooth. Salt and pepper to taste.

3. Put half of the butter in the snail shells. Put the snails in the shells and top with the rest of the butter.

4. Put the snails on a baking sheet, and bake for 10 minutes. Serve immediately.

Nutritional Info: Calories: 244 | Sodium: 264mg | Dietary Fiber: 0.6g | Total Fat: 23.4g | Total Carbs: 2.4g | Protein: 7.0g.

BUFFALO CHICKEN BALLS

Servings: 8 | Prep Time: 30 Minutes | Cook Time: 3 Minutes

INGREDIENTS

4 cups cooked chicken

4 ounces cream cheese

1/2 cup hot sauce

3/4 teaspoons garlic powder

1/2 teaspoons onion powder

1-3/4 cups shredded cheddar cheese

2 quarts vegetable oil

1 cup flour

3 whole eggs

2 cups panko bread crumbs

Imagine all the taste of buffalo chicken wings or dip in a bite sized form. They're fast and easy to make, and will be a hit at your next tailgate or party.

DIRECTIONS

1. Put the cream cheese out to soften.

2. Put the chicken in your food processor, and pulse it until the chicken is finely chopped. Place the chicken in a bowl to be used later.

3. Put the cream cheese in your food processor, and pulse until the cream cheese becomes smooth. Put in the onion powder, garlic powder, 1/4 cup of hot sauce, and pulse again until the mixture is smooth. Add more hot sauce to taste if necessary.

4. Mixture together the chicken and cream cheese mixture, until well combined. Form the mixture into 3/4 to 1-inch balls. Put the balls on a baking sheet lined with wax paper.

5. Heat the oil to 350F in a large pot. Get out 3 small pans, fill the first with flour and salt and pepper to taste, in the second pan whisk together the water and egg, and put the bread crumbs in the 3rd.

6. Roll the balls around in each pan until the balls are completely covered, starting with the 1st and ending with the 3rd.

7. Carefully put the balls in the oil, and fry until golden brown, around 2-3 minutes. Let the balls drain on a paper towel.

8. Serve with the dip of your choice.

Nutritional Info: Calories: 402 | Sodium: 776mg | Dietary Fiber: 1.7g | Total Fat: 15.0g | Total Carbs: 32.6g | Protein: 32.3g.

SWEET AND SOUR CHICKEN EGG ROLLS

Servings: 16 Egg Rolls | Prep Time: 25 Minutes | Cook Time: 15 Minutes

INGREDIENTS

16 egg roll wrappers

Vegetable oil, for frying

CHICKEN EGG ROLL FILLING:

1 tablespoon olive oil

1 pound boneless skinless chicken breasts

1/2 onion

2 cloves garlic

1 (12-ounce) package stir-fry vegetables (snow peas, carrots, broccoli, bean sprouts)

1 red bell pepper

1 cup pineapple (from 1 can 20-ounce pineapple chunks in juice)

SWEET AND SOUR SAUCE:

1/4 cup pineapple juice

1/2 cup red wine vinegar

3/4 cups sugar

3 tablespoons ketchup

1 tablespoons soy sauce

1/2 teaspoon salt

1/4 teaspoon ginger powder

1/2 teaspoon hot red chili sauce

2 teaspoons cornstarch

These have all the delicious flavor of sweet and sour chicken in a bite sized form. Prep time is a breeze because you don't have to worry about mincing vegetables. You just throw them in your food processor, and let it do the work for you.

Nutritional Info: Calories: 688 | Sodium: 347mg | Dietary Fiber: 1.0g | Total Fat: 57.9g | Total Carbs: 31.9g | Protein: 11.6g.

DIRECTIONS

1. Cut the chicken into thin strips. Chop the onion. Core and slice the bell pepper

2. Put all of the sweet and sour sauce ingredients in a medium sauce pan, and whisk them together.

3. Bring the mixture up to a boil, and then lower the heat to let it simmer until the sauce starts to thicken. The sauce will thicken while it cools.

4. Heat 1 tablespoon of oil on high heat in a large skillet. Put in the onions and chicken, let them cook until the chicken is almost completely cooked.

5. Then lower the heat to medium-high, put in the pineapple and vegetable, and cook for about 3 minutes. The chicken should be totally cooked, and the vegetables should be tender-crisp. Mix in 1/4 cup of the sweet and sour sauce.

6. Put the mixture in your food processor using a slotted spoon. Pulse until the ingredients are finely chopped.

7. Take out one of the wrappers, and have one point facing you. Take 1/4 cup of the mixture and place it in the center of the bottom third or so of the wrapper.

8. Take the bottom corner and fold it over the filling, and then continue to fold. Fold the sides over the center of the filling as you're folding. Use water to get the top corner moist, and seal the eggroll. Repeat the process until you run out of filling.

9. Use a deep pot to heat oil to 350F, and put the egg rolls in up to 4 at a time. Turn them throughout frying. Allow egg rolls to drain on a paper towel when they're crispy. And golden brown.

10. Serve with remaining sweet and sour sauce. Mix in a little water if sauce is too thick.

CHAPTER
9

MAIN DISHES

ARROZ CON POLLO

Servings: 8 | Prep Time: 20 Minutes | Cook Time: 1 Hour 10 Minutes

INGREDIENTS

8 skinless chicken thighs

1 tablespoon vinegar

2 teaspoons sazon

1/2 teaspoon adobo powder

1/2 garlic powder

3 teaspoons olive oil

1/2 onion

1/4 cup cilantro

3 cloves garlic

5 scallions

2 tablespoons bell pepper

1 tomato

2-1/2 cups enriched long grain rice

4 cups water

1 chicken bouillon cube

Salt to taste (about 2 teaspoon)

Arroz con pollo is a one dish meal that your entire family will love. It consists of chicken and rice, with variations that sometimes add olives. It gets its exotic flavor from the adobo and sazon.

Nutritional Info: Calories: 380 | Sodium: 350mg | Dietary Fiber: 1.3g | Total Fat: 7.8g | Total Carbs: 48.6g | Protein: 26.3g.

DIRECTIONS

1. Dice the tomato. Use 1/2 teaspoon of sazon, vinegar, and adobo to season the chicken on both sides. Allow the seasoned chicken to rest for at least 10 minutes.

2. Heat 2 teaspoons of oil on medium heat in a medium skillet. Add in the seasoned chicken, and let it cook for 5 minutes per side, until it browns, then set aside chicken.

3. Put the pepper, onions, scallions, and garlic in your food processor, and process on speed 1 until finely chopped.

4. Put the rest of the oil in the skillet, heat on medium-low heat, and transfer the mixture from your food processor to the skillet.

5. Cook the mixture for around 3 minutes, until the onions become soft. Put in the tomato, and cook for an additionally minute.

6. Mix and cook for an additional minute before putting in the bouillon cube, water, and the rest of the sazon.

7. Make sure the bouillon dissolves completely, and scrape off any browned pieces from the bottom of the pan. Salt to taste.

8. Put the chicken in the mixture and make sure it's well packed into the rice. Bring the mixture to a boil, and then let it simmer on medium-low until most of the water disappears.

9. When the water is around the rice line and bubbling, cover, and lower to the heat to low.

10. Let the dish cook covered for 20 minutes without being disturbed, then take it off the heat and let it sit for an additional 10 minutes. Use a fork to fluff the rice before serving.

BAKED SEABASS WITH GARLIC BUTTER AND BREADCRUMB TOPPING

> Servings: 4 | Prep Time: 20 Minutes | Cook Time: 15 Minutes

INGREDIENTS

5-ounce sourdough bread

1 tablespoon butter, plus 1/2 stick unsalted butter

4 (6-ounce) sea bass, fillets

Salt and freshly ground black pepper

1 lemon, zested and juiced

Few sprigs thyme, leaves removed

3 cloves garlic, smashed

1 cup fresh parsley leaves

The full flavor of the garlic butter complements the rich flavor of the seabass. The breadcrumbs add a lovely contrast of texture to the fish.

DIRECTIONS

1. Remove the leaves from the thyme sprigs. Smash the garlic cloves. Preheat your oven to 350F. Grease a large casserole dish with one tablespoon of butter.

2. Put the bread in your food process, and pulse it until it becomes coarse bread crumbs.

3. Put the fish in the casserole dish, salt and pepper to taste, and add the thyme, lemon zest and juice.

4. In a large skillet, on medium heat, melt a 1/2-stick of butter with the garlic. Let the ingredients cook until the butter starts to bubble. Then turn off the heat and allow the ingredients to continue to meld.

5. After a few minutes, remove the garlic from the butter. Put the bread crumbs in the skillet, and mix until all the butter is absorbed. Mix in the parsley, and salt and pepper to taste.

6. Layer the bread crumbs on top of the fish. Bake for about 12 to 15 minutes. The fish should be completely cooked, and the breadcrumbs should be golden.

7. Serve immediately.

Nutritional Info: Calories: 592 | Sodium: 341mg | Dietary Fiber: 3.3g | Total Fat: 36g | Total Carbs: 23.7g | Protein: 43.7g.

BARCELONA CHICKEN

Servings: 4 | Prep Time: At least 4 Hours | Cook Time: 30-40 Minutes

INGREDIENTS

MARINADE:

5 scallions, cut into 1-inch pieces

1 cup lightly packed fresh basil leaves

3 large garlic cloves

2 serrano chili peppers, roughly chopped

1?4 cup extra-virgin olive oil

2 tablespoons sherry vinegar

1 teaspoon kosher salt

1/2 teaspoon freshly ground black pepper

1 whole chicken, 4 to 5 pounds

This Spanish influence chicken gets a ton of flavor from being marinated ahead of time. This also cuts down on the overall prep time. Marinate the chicken overnight for maximum flavor.

DIRECTIONS

1. Cut the scallions into 1 inch pieces. Roughly chop the serrano chilies.

2. Put all the marinade ingredients in your food processor and process on speed 2 until a smooth paste is formed.

3. Cut up the chicken. Cut it into 2 wings, 2 breast, 2 thighs, and 2 legs. If desired cut the breasts in half. Put the pieces in a large plastic bag, and add the marinade. Seal the bag, making sure there's no excess air. Turn the bag upside down, and shake it around, until the chicken is covered in marinade.

4. Put the bag in a bowl and then in the refrigerator. Let the chicken marinate for at least for hours, and up to 24 hours. Turn the bag occasionally.

5. Set the grill for medium heat.

6. Take the chicken out of the bag, and throw out the bag with marinade.

7. Grill the chicken with the skin side down, on indirect heat at first. During the last 10 minutes of cooking, move the chicken onto direct heat.

8. Take the chicken off the grill when it's fully cooked, and brown.

9. Serve the chicken while it's still hot.

Nutritional Info: Calories: 984 | Sodium: 395mg | Dietary Fiber: 0.8g | Total Fat: 46.3g | Total Carbs: 2.8g | Protein: 132.0g.

BEEF CARPACCIO

Servings: 6 | Prep Time: 10 Minutes | Cook Time: 10 Minutes

INGREDIENTS

400-gram piece center cut fillet of beef

200 grams each yellow and green beans, stem end trimmed

Caper berries for garnish

Chervil or parsley

Parmesan for shaving

Sea salt and ground pepper

DRESSING:

1/3 cup olive oil

1 teaspoon tarragon vinegar

1 tablespoon capers

1 clove garlic, crushed

1 teaspoon Dijon mustard

1 teaspoon dried tarragon

Small handful basil leaves

1/2 cup freshly grated parmesan cheese

This dish relies on using a very high quality piece of beef. This is one time to splurge. The caper dressing compliments the rich taste of the raw beef well.

DIRECTIONS

1. Trim, remove the stems from the beans, and cut the lengthwise.

2. Put all of the dressing ingredients in your food processor and process on speed 2 until completely smooth.

3. Boil salted water in a medium pot, and add the beans. Cook them until they start to become tender. Then remove them from the boiling water and run them under cold water. Dry them, and mix with the dressing.

4. Carefully cut the meat into very thin slices. Put the slice in the middle of two pieces of plastic wrap and flatten it with a rolling pin.

5. Plate the meat, top it with the beans, then garnish with the dressing, parsley or chervil, parmesan, and capers.

Nutritional Info: Calories: 265 | Sodium: 162mg | Dietary Fiber: 2.4g | Total Fat: 16.9g | Total Carbs: 5.4g | Protein: 23.8g.

BEET BURGER WITH CITRUS CAPER AIOLI

Servings: 4 | Prep Time: 25 Minutes | Cook Time: 30 Minutes

INGREDIENTS

4 tablespoons grapeseed oil

1 medium yellow onion

2 cups cooked brown rice

1 cup raw red beets

1 cup walnuts

1/2 cup yellow raisins

1/2 teaspoon granulated garlic

2 large eggs

Bibb lettuce leaves, for serving

CITRUS-CAPER AIOLI:

1/2 cup mayonnaise

2 tablespoons capers

1 tablespoon honey mustard

1 teaspoon orange zest plus 2 tablespoons fresh orange juice

Kosher salt and freshly ground black pepper, optional

These burgers are a great meatless alternative for vegetarians. The beets have a nice earthly flavor that's balanced out by the citrusy, creamy flavor of the aioli.

DIRECTIONS

1. Mince the onion. Peel and roughly chop the beats. Cool the brown rice if it's hot.

2. Combine the aioli ingredient in a bowl, and salt and pepper to taste.

3. Heat 2 tablespoons of oil on medium heat in a pan. Put in the onion, and salt and pepper to taste. Cook the onion until they start to turn golden, around 10 minutes. Let cool.

4. Put the granulated garlic, brown rice, cooled onions, beets, raisins and walnuts in your food processor.

5. Pulse the ingredients until they resemble ground meat, about 10 times. Put the mixture in a bowl, add 1 teaspoon of salt, pepper to taste, and the egg. Use your hand to mix the ingredients until well combined.

6. Make 4 tightly packed patties out of the mixture. Salt and pepper both sides of the patties.

7. Heat 2 tablespoons of oil in a non-stick pan. Once the oil is heated, place the patties in the pan, and cook for around 10 minutes per side.

8. The patties should be brown and crispy before flipping. Don't move the patties around while cooking, simply flip once. Put the patties on hamburger buns, or the lettuces leaves, and top with the aioli. Serve while still hot.

Nutritional Info: Calories: 905 | Sodium: 431mg | Dietary Fiber: 7.7g | Total Fat: 47.1g | Total Carbs: 106.7g | Protein: 19.9g.

CHICKEN NUGGETS

Servings: 42 Nuggets | Prep Time: 40 Minutes | Cook Time: 8 Minutes

INGREDIENTS

3 boneless skinless chicken breasts

1-1/2 teaspoons of salt

3/4 teaspoons of parsley flakes

3/4 teaspoons of oregano

1/4 (heaping) teaspoon of onion powder

1/4 (heaping) teaspoon of pepper

3 eggs

1-1/2 cups of flour

1-1/2 teaspoons salt

2 cups of canola oil

Now you can make this kid favorite at home with all the same flavor that you find in a restaurant. The advantage of making them at home is you know exactly what's going into the nuggets. There are no harmful additives or chemicals.

DIRECTIONS

1. Mix the oregano, parsley, onion powder, salt, and pepper in a small bowl. Beat the eggs and set aside.

2. Place the oil in a heavy skillet with a candy thermometer attached, and heat on medium-high heat.

3. While heating, cube the chicken and put it in your food processor. Process on speed 1 until the chicken resembles a paste. Then put the chicken in a bowl.

4. Season the chicken with herb mixture you created, then mix well.

5. Mix the flour and salt well, and put it on a large plate.

6. Use a cookie scoop to make 42 balls out of the chicken.

7. Roll the balls in the flour, then dip them in the beaten eggs then back in the flour. Push the balls down to create a nugget shape.

8. Check on the oil and temperature, and put the nuggets in the oil in batches when the temperature reaches between 350F-365F.

9. Let the nuggets fry until the bottom sides is golden, then flip and repeat. It should take between 4-5 minutes per side.

10. Drain nuggets on paper towels. Serve hot.

Nutritional Info: Calories: 161 | Sodium: 619mg | Dietary Fiber: 0g | Total Fat: 11.0g | Total Carbs: 12.6g | Protein: 2.8g.

CILANTRO LIME FLANK STEAK TACOS

Servings: 4 | Prep Time: 35 Minutes | Cook Time: 12-20 Minutes

INGREDIENTS

FOR THE MARINADE:

1 (2-pound) flank steak

1/3 cup olive oil

1 lime, juiced

1 garlic clove, smashed

A handful of cilantro

2 teaspoons of honey

1/2 teaspoon of cumin

1/2 teaspoon of ancho-chili pepper

1/2 teaspoon red pepper flakes

Kosher salt and fresh black pepper, to taste

FOR THE STEAK TACOS:

2 pounds prepared cilantro-lime marinated flank steak

10-12 soft flour tortillas

Iceberg lettuce

Pico de gallo

Grated Monterey jack cheese

These tasty tacos get their flavor from the cilantro lime marinade. The citrus flavor from the marinade compliments the rich flavor of the beef.

DIRECTIONS

1. Smash the garlic, and shred or slice the lettuce.

2. Place the garlic, lime juice, and cilantro in your food processor and pulse until ingredients are chopped. Put in the rest of the marinade ingredients and pulse until ingredients are mixed together.

3. Put the steak on a plate on the counter and completely cover with the marinade. Allow the steak to marinate for at least 30 Minutes.

4. Grill on medium-high heat for about 6-10 minutes a side depending on how well you like your steak cooked.

5. Thinly slice the steak. Make tacos using meat, and a mix of the lettuce, pico de gallo, and cheese.

Nutritional Info: Calories: 762 | Sodium: 168mg | Dietary Fiber: 5.2g | Total Fat: 37.9g | Total Carbs: 37.3g | Protein: 67.7g.

DAIRY-FREE STUFFED SHELLS

Servings: 6-8 | Prep Time: 20 Minutes | Cook Time: 45 Minutes

INGREDIENTS

2 tablespoons olive oil

1-1/2 teaspoons salt

1 teaspoon oregano

16 ounces tofu

2 cloves garlic

1 tablespoon nutritional yeast

10 ounces frozen spinach

1 box jumbo shells

1 jar marinara sauce

These are just like the stuffed shells you grew up with, but with tofu instead of cheese. Processing the tofu in your food processor gives it the same texture as ricotta cheese.

DIRECTIONS

1. Defrost the spinach. Drain the tofu, dry it using a paper tower and crumble it. Preheat the oven to 350F.

2. Put the tofu, salt, olive oil, oregano, nutritional yeast, and garlic in your food processor. Process on speed 2 until the tofu has a similar texture to ricotta cheese.

3. Mix the tofu mixture with the spinach. Boil the shells in salted water until they're al dente. When al dente drain the shells.

4. Cover the bottom of a 9x13 pan with around 1/2 cup of pasta sauce. Use 2 tablespoons of the tofu mixture to fill the shells, and place them in the pan with the seam side down.

5. Pour the rest of the sauce on the shells, cover the pan, and bake for 30 Minutes. Serve the shells hot.

Nutritional Info: Calories: 312.5 | Sodium: 808mg | Dietary Fiber: 5.3g | Total Fat: 9.0g | Total Carbs: 45.9g | Protein: 12.9g.

GRILLED LOBSTER TAILS WITH NECTARINE LIME SAUCE

Servings: 4 | Prep Time: 5 Minutes | Cook Time: 10 Minutes

INGREDIENTS

4 (1/2 pound each) lobster tails

2 (about 1/2 pound) nectarines

1 scallion

Juice of 3 limes

2 tablespoons extra-virgin olive oil

1/2 teaspoons sea salt

1/4 teaspoons habanero pepper

1 lime (for garnish)

This a very fast dish to prepare that's full of flavor. The rich flavor of the lobster is perfectly complimented by the sweet and citrusy flavor off the sauce.

DIRECTIONS

1. Peel and slice the nectarines. Chop the scallion. Quarter the lime. Finely mince and deseed the habanero. Heat your grill to medium-high heat

2. Put the habanero, scallion, nectarine, 2 tablespoons of lime juice, 1 tablespoon of olive oil, and 1/4 teaspoon of salt. Process on speed 2 until ingredients are pureed. Put the sauce in a bowl.

3. Whisk the rest of the lime juice, salt, and olive oil together in a bowl.

4. Open up the lobster tails lengthwise, and if you prefer, remove the membrane. Cover the lobster meat with the lime juice mixture using a brush.

5. Grill the tails with the meat side down for 4 minutes. Then flip over and grill for 4 to 5 more minutes, until the meat turns opaque.

6. Serve with a side of the nectarine sauce.

Nutritional Info: Calories: 304 | Sodium: 1338mg | Dietary Fiber: 2.5g | Total Fat: 9.2g | Total Carbs: 11.6g | Protein: 44.1g.

GRILLED SALMON WITH HERBED YOGURT SAUCE

Servings: 2 | Prep Time: 15 Minutes | Cook Time: 10 Minutes

INGREDIENTS

FRESH HERB YOGURT SAUCE:

1 cup watercress

1/4 cup cilantro

1/4 cup mint

1 scallion

1 cup low-fat yogurt

1 tablespoon fresh lime juice

Sea salt and fresh ground pepper, to taste

GRILLED SALMON:

8 ounces fresh salmon filet

1 teaspoon olive oil

Sea salt and fresh ground pepper

The salmon and yogurt sauce create a wonderful, light meal. It's perfect for hot summer nights, especially when you don't feel like spending a long time in the kitchen,

DIRECTIONS

1. Chop up the scallion.
2. Put the cilantro, scallion, mint, and watercress in your food processor, and process on speed 1 until the ingredients are minced.
3. Put in the yogurt and lime juice, and process again, on speed one, until well mixed with green dots still visible.
4. Salt and pepper to taste.
5. Massage the salmon with olive oil, and salt and pepper to taste. Grill the salmon for about 5 minutes per side. Serve with a nice helping of yogurt sauce.

Nutritional Info: Calories: 270 | Sodium: 152mg | Dietary Fiber: 1.3g | Total Fat: 11.0g | Total Carbs: 10.9g | Protein: 30.1g.

MUGHLAI CHICKEN

Servings: 8 | Prep Time: 30 Minutes | Cook Time: 20 Minutes

INGREDIENTS

3 pounds boned chicken thighs

1 (1-inch) piece ginger

4 cloves garlic

2 teaspoons ground cumin

1 teaspoon ground coriander

1/2 teaspoon dried chili flakes

4 tablespoons ground almonds

1/2 cup water

5 cardamom pods, bruised

1 cinnamon stick

2 bay leaves

4 cloves garlic

1/4 cup vegetable oil

2 onions, finely chopped

1 cup yogurt

1 cup chicken stock

1/2 cup heavy cream

1/2 cup raisins

1 teaspoon garam masala

1 tablespoon sugar

1 teaspoon salt

3/4 cups flaked almonds, toasted, to garnish

This Indian chicken dish has a rich flavor with notes of exotic spices. This dish's roots are in Central Asia but made its way to India centuries ago.

DIRECTIONS

1. Cut the chicken thighs into 2 pieces. Peel the garlic, and ginger. Bruise the cardamom pods. Break the cinnamon stick in half.

2. Put the garlic, cumin, ginger, chili, and coriander in your food processor, and process on speed 1 until a paste is formed.

3. Then add in the almonds and water, and process on speed 2 until well combined.

4. In a large pan, heat the oil on medium heat, and then add the chicken in batches. Cook the chicken until both sides are sealed. Take the chicken out of the pan.

5. Put the cinnamon stick, bay leaf, and cardamom pods in the pan, and mix them with the oil. Put in the onions, stir frequently, and let them cook until become brown and start to soften.

6. Add in the paste, and continue to cook until the paste changes color. Slowly mix the yogurt in in half cup intervals. Then mix in the cream, sultanas, and stock.

7. Add the chicken back in the pan, then top it with the sugar, salt, and gran masala. Let the mixture cook for 20 minutes, on low heat, covered. Make sure the chicken is totally cooked before removing from heat.

8. Garnish with toasted almost and serve.

Nutritional Info: Calories: 486 | Sodium: 561mg | Dietary Fiber: 1.7g | Total Fat: 24.4g | Total Carbs: 11.7g | Protein: 52.7g.

PORK CHOPS WITH TZATZIKI AND ROMESCO SAUCE

Servings: 2 | Prep Time: 1 Hour 20 Minutes | Cook Time: 30 Minutes

INGREDIENTS

MARINATED PORK FILLET:

1 teaspoon ground turmeric

1 teaspoon ground paprika

1 teaspoon ground ginger

1 teaspoon ground cumin

Splash sesame oil

2 tablespoons brown sugar

1 tablespoon Worcestershire sauce

1 teaspoon chili powder

1 teaspoon tomato paste

1 teaspoon salt

1/2 teaspoon black pepper

7 ounces pork fillet

Splash olive oil

TZATZIKI:

1 cucumber

1 teaspoon salt

7 ounces greek yoghurt

1 clove garlic, chopped

1 handful mint leaves, chopped

Salt and black pepper

Tzatziki is Greek yogurt based sauce that gives a creaminess to the pork. Romesco is Spanish red pepper based sauce that adds delicious complex flavor.

ROMESCO SAUCE:

1 red pepper

1 red onion, chopped

2 chilies, deseeded and halved lengthwise

2 tablespoons olive oil

2 plum tomatoes

4-1/2 ounces almonds, ground

1 tablespoon white wine vinegar

4 anchovy fillets in oil

1 ounce white bread

4-1/2 ounces olive oil, toasted and crust removed

Salt and pepper

Nutritional Info: Calories: 754 | Sodium: 753mg | Dietary Fiber: 8.1g | Total Fat: 60.6g | Total Carbs: 32.6g | Protein: 26.6g.

DIRECTIONS

1. Peel, seed, and finely chop the cucumber.

2. Preheat your oven to 400F.

3. Combine the cucumbers and salt, then let them rest in a colander for 1 hour. Then use a paper towel to pat them dry.

4. Place the pork marinade ingredients, except the olive oil, in a bowl and combine. Then put in the pork fillets, and cover them completely with the marinade. Let the pork marinate for 30 minutes.

5. Heat the splash of olive oil on medium heat in a frying pan. Cook the marinated pork chops for 1 to minutes per side.

6. Put the pork in the oven, and cook for 8 to 10 minutes. The pork should be completely cooked. Let the pork rest in a warm place for 5 minutes.

7. Put the cucumbers in a bowl, and combine with the yogurt, mint, and garlic. Salt and pepper to taste.

8. Put the onions, olive oil, chilies, and pepper in a roasting tray, and roast in the oven for 8-10 minutes. The chilies, and onions have softened and are brown.

9. While the vegetables are roasting, heat a frying pan on medium heat until it's hot. Once hot, sear the tomatoes cut side down, until they've blackened.

10. Put the bread, anchovies, ground almonds, vinegar, and roasted vegetables in your food processor. Process for 2 minutes on speed 1 until the mixture is smooth. While the machine is still running, slowly add in 4 1/2 ounces of olive oil, continue to process until well incorporated.

11. Salt and pepper to taste.

12. Serve the pork chop sliced, with dollop of romesco, and tzatziki on each side.

STEAK SANDWICHES

Servings: 4 | Prep Time: 10 Minutes | Cook Time: 15 Minutes

INGREDIENTS

2 tablespoons ketchup

1 tablespoon Dijon mustard

1 jarred hot cherry pepper

1 teaspoon red wine vinegar

1 pound beef sirloin tips (flap meat)

Kosher salt and freshly ground black pepper

3 tablespoons olive oil

1 small yellow onion

6 ounces white mushrooms

1-1/2 cups shredded sharp Cheddar

4 long rolls, split and lightly toasted

1-1/2 ounce baby arugula

You use your food processor to get the steak into finely sliced little pieces. The steak gets a delicious flavor from the ketchup, mustard, and peppers mixture that it's cooked in.

Nutritional Info: Calories: 433 | Sodium: 733mg | Dietary Fiber: 1.4g | Total Fat: 21.6g | Total Carbs: 12.2g | Protein: 47.4g.

DIRECTIONS

1. Slice the mushroom. Cut the steak into 1-inch pieces. Stem, seed, and chop the cherry peppers. Halve, and thinly slice the onion.

2. Combine the vinegar, peppers, mustard, and ketchup in a bowl, and set aside.

3. Pulse half the steak in your food processor until chopped. Then do the same thing with the other half of the steak.

4. Season the steak with 1/2 teaspoon of salt and pepper. Toss the steak to make sure it's well coated.

5. Use a heavy skillet to heat 1-1/2 tablespoons of oil on medium-high heat. Put in the steak, cooking for around 3 minutes, until the steak has lost the majority of its original color, stir occasionally throughout. Remove the steak from the skillet.

6. In a pan, heat the rest of the oil on medium heat. Put in 1/4 teaspoon of salt and the onions, cooking for around 4 minutes, making sure to stir frequently until the onions are beginning to soften, and become brown.

7. Next, put in the mushrooms and an additional 1/4 teaspoon of salt, cooking for around another 2 minutes, until the mushrooms start releasing their liquid and become soft, stir frequently throughout.

8. Put in the vinegar mixture, and steak. Stir frequently for around 2 minutes until the meat is warmed up. Mix in the cheese until it melts completely.

9. Toast, and cut the rolls lengthwise. Put in the steak mixture, and top with arugula.

10. Serve immediately.

TEA SMOKED SHRIMP WITH ASIAN PESTO AND VEGETABLE RIBBON SALAD

Servings: 2 | Prep Time: 25 Minutes | Cook Time: 10 Minutes

INGREDIENTS

TEA SMOKED SHRIMP:

3/4 pounds jumbo shrimp

1/4 cup long grain rice

1/4 cup loose black tea

2 tablespoons dark brown sugar

1 teaspoon vegetable oil

VEGETABLE RIBBON SALAD:

2 garlic cloves

2 medium carrots

1 medium parsnip

1 medium broccoli stem (longer the better)

Salt to taste

This recipe sounds a lot more complex than it actually is. Each step is easy to do. Make sure you open all your kitchen windows and vent your stove when you smoke the shrimp.

ASIAN PESTO:

4 garlic cloves

1-inch knob of ginger

1/2 cup roasted peanuts

1/2 cup packed basil

1/4 cup packed fresh mint

1/4 cup packed cilantro

1/4 cup packed parsley

2 tablespoons fresh squeezed lemon juice

1 teaspoon fish sauce

1/2 cup olive oil

2 tablespoons toasted sesame oil

Salt and pepper to taste

Nutritional Info: Calories: 656 | Sodium: 415mg | Dietary Fiber: 9.1g | Total Fat: 44.2g | Total Carbs: 40.7g | Protein: 31.0g.

DIRECTIONS

1. Peel the ginger, garlic, carrots, and parsnip. Mince the garlic. Peel and devein the shrimp. Trim the broccoli stem.

2. Line the wok with a single piece of aluminum foil to cover the bottom and sides of the wok. Make sure there's no space between the wok and the aluminum foil. Put on a second layer of the same size aluminum foil crosswise.

3. Place the jasmine rice in the bottom of the wok. Place the black tea on top of the rice. Put the brown sugar on top of the tea. Put a 10-inch wire cake rack in the bottom of the wok. Carefully grease the wire rack with vegetable oil.

4. Put the shrimp on the rack and cover with a lid. Use aluminum foil to cover the wok if you don't have a lid that fits. Make sure the shrimp doesn't touch the foil and has enough room to let the smoke rise and smoke the shrimp.

5. Turn on the heat to high until the smoking ingredients start to smoke, around 1-2 minutes. Turn the heat down to medium-low and smoke for 8 minutes until the shrimp are firm, and have an orange color.

6. Let them smoke a little longer if 8 minutes isn't enough. Take rack with shrimp and let it cool on a plate. Throw out the smoking ingredients, and foil WHEN ingredients have cooled.

7. Make long ribbons out of the parsnips, broccoli, and carrots using a peeler. Fill a large pot with heavily salted water. Bring it to a boil.

8. While the water is boiling. Place ice and cold water in a medium bowl. When the water is boiling add the vegetable ribbons, and boil for 1 minute. Remove the ribbons and place them directly in the ice bath for 2 minutes.

9. Drain the bowl, keeping the ribbons in the bowl, and place a damp paper towel on top of the bowl.

10. Put all of the pesto ingredient except for the salt and pepper in your food processor. Process on speed 2 until a paste is formed. Then salt and pepper to taste.

11. Place the vegetable ribbons on a plate, then add a spoonful of the pesto, and top with the shrimp.

12. Serve immediately.

VEGGIE LENTIL LOAF

Servings: 8 | Prep Time: 30 Minutes | Cook Time: 1 Hour 40 Minutes

INGREDIENTS

LOAF:

1 cup dry lentils

2-1/2 cups water or vegetable broth

3 tablespoons flaxseed meal

1/3 cup water

2 tablespoons olive oil

3 garlic cloves

1 small onion

1 small red bell pepper

1 carrot

1 celery stalk

3/4 cup oats

1/2 cup oat flour

1 heaping teaspoon dried thyme

1/2 heaping teaspoon cumin

1/2 teaspoon garlic powder

1/2 teaspoon onion powder

1/4 – 1/2 teaspoon ground chipotle pepper, optional

Cracked pepper & sea salt to taste

GLAZE:

3 tablespoons ketchup

1 tablespoon balsamic vinegar

1 tablespoon maple syrup

This loaf has the same great texture as meatloaf, but with loads of veggies. Try changing the vegetables if you don't like the ones in the recipe.

DIRECTIONS

1. Mince the garlic, and finely dice the onions, celery, carrots, and bell peppers. Rinse the lentils. Preheat you oven to 350F. Line a loaf pan with parchment paper.

2. Bring the lentils and 2-1/2 cups of water to a boil in a large pot. Lower the heat, and let the lentils simmer, covered for around 40 minutes. Stir occasionally, and let the lentils cool for about 15 minutes with the liquid.

3. While the lentils are cooling, mix the flax meal, and 1/3 cup of water. Let the mixture rest in the refrigerator for 10 minutes.

4. Heat the water or oil on medium heat in a pan. Cook the celery, carrots, garlic, onions, and bell pepper for around 5 minutes. Mix in the spices while cooking. Once cooked, let the vegetables cool.

5. Put 3/4 of the lentils in your food processor, and process on speed 1, until well blended.

6. Mix the lentils, veggies, oats, flax water mixture, and flour, until well combined. Salt and pepper to taste. Put the meatloaf mixture in the lined loaf pan. Pack it down so that it reaches into the corners.

7. Mix all the glaze ingredient in a bowl. Put the glaze on top of the meatloaf. Bake the meatloaf for 45 to 50 minutes. Allow the meatloaf to cool off a bit before slicing, and serving.

Nutritional Info: Calories: 206 | Sodium: 77mg | Dietary Fiber: 10.1g | Total Fat: 5.6g | Total Carbs: 30.4g | Protein: 9.0g.

ALAMBRE DE CAMARONES

Servings: 4 | Prep Time: 20 Minutes | Cook Time: 10 Minutes

INGREDIENTS

MARINADE:

2 cloves garlic, smashed

1 tablespoon olive oil

2 tablespoons fresh lime juice

1 teaspoon Worcestershire sauce

1 teaspoon dried oregano

1/2 teaspoon salt

1/4 teaspoon black pepper, ground

SHRIMP:

8 bamboo skewers

24 large shrimp

16 serrano chilies

1 small red onion

24 cherry tomatoes

This is a deliciously tangy shrimp dish. It packs some heat from the chilies, and is ready in under 30 minutes.

DIRECTIONS

1. Peel and devein the shrimp. Slice the onion into 8 wedges, and then slice them lengthwise into thirds. Soak the bamboo skewers in water for 30 minutes, Smash the garlic.

2. Place all of the marinade ingredients in your food processor and puree on speed 2 until completely smooth.

3. Toss the shrimp in the marinade until they're well-covered. Let the shrimp marinate in the refrigerator for at least 10 minutes or up to 2 hours.

4. Put one chili on each skewer, then 1 shrimp, a tomato, and an onion wedge. Repeat the shrimp through onion section twice per skewer and finish with a 2nd pepper. Salt the skewers to taste.

5. Heat your grill to high. Grill the skewers for around 5 minutes per side. The onions should have a nice char, and the shrimp are completely cooked.

Nutritional Info: Calories: 313 | Sodium: 618mg | Dietary Fiber: 9.6g | Total Fat: 7.0g | Total Carbs: 34.0g | Protein: 32.7g.

CHAPTER

10

SNACKS

BLACK BEAN BURGERS
WITH PICO DE GALLO

Servings: 4 | Prep Time: 15 Minutes | Cook Time: 10 Minutes

INGREDIENTS

BURGERS:

2 cans of black beans

1 medium onion

2 garlic cloves

2 tablespoons cilantro

1 small jalapeno

2 teaspoons cumin

2 teaspoons chili powder

1/8 teaspoon allspice

1 egg beaten

1/2 cup chickpea flour

Olive oil

PICO DE GALLO:

3 roma tomatoes

1 small onion

1 small jalapeno

2 tablespoons cilantro

1 teaspoon red wine vinegar

1/4 teaspoon chili powder

1 teaspoon lime juice

Dash of sugar

These burgers are a great vegetarian alternative to a regular burger. They're packed with protein and fiber, and have a great southwestern flavor

DIRECTIONS

1. Drain and rinse the black beans. Chop the cilantro, and mince the garlic. Core, seed, and dice the jalapenos. Dice the onion for the pico de gallo, and finely dice the onion for the burgers. Dice the tomatoes.

2. Mix all of the pico de gallo ingredients in a bowl, and refrigerate.

3. Put the jalapeno, beans, garlic, onion, and cilantro in your food processor. Pulse until the ingredients have a thick dough consistency.

4. Put in the egg, allspice, cumin, chili powder, and flour. Pulse the ingredients again until they are thoroughly combined. Make sure the ingredients don't turn into a puree. They should still be chunky. Transfer the mixture to a bowl, and refrigerate for 20 minutes.

5. After they mixture has been chilled, form it into 4 patties.

6. In a non-stick skillet heat olive oil on medium heat, and cook the burgers for around 5 minutes per side.

7. Top the burgers with the pico de gallo and serve.

Nutritional Info: Calories: 349 | Sodium: 48mg | Dietary Fiber: 15.9g | Total Fat: 4.2g | Total Carbs: 60.8g | Protein: 20.4g.

BUTTERMILK BISCUITS

Servings: 10-12 Biscuits | Prep Time: 10 Minutes | Bake Time: 10 Minutes

INGREDIENTS

2 cups unbleached all¬-purpose flour

1/4 teaspoon baking soda 1

1 tablespoon baking powder

1 teaspoon kosher salt

6 tablespoons unsalted butter

1 cup buttermilk

These biscuits are delicious, and tender. Using the processor to mix the dough actually helps to make them more tender.

DIRECTIONS

1. Preheat your oven to 450F.

2. Put all of the dry ingredients in your food processor. Then out in the butter and pulse, until a coarse meal is formed.

3. Add in the buttermilk and pulse until all ingredients are just combined. The dough should be wet. Add more buttermilk if the dough is dry.

4. Put the dough on a floured surface, such as a cutting board.

5. Pat the dough carefully until the dough becomes 1/2-inch thick. Once 1/2-inch thick, fold the dough, keep folding the dough until it's been folded 5 times. Then press the dough down carefully, until it's 1 inch thick.

6. Use a round object such as a can, or biscuit cutter to cut out the biscuits.

7. Put the biscuits on a baking sheet touching each other if you like soft biscuits. Put them on the baking sheet 1 inch apart if you like crispier biscuits.

8. If desired, brush the biscuits with a little milk, and top with freshly cracked pepper.

9. Bake the biscuits for 10-12 minutes.

Nutritional Info: Calories: 136 | Sodium: 285mg | Dietary Fiber: 0.6g | Total Fat: 6.1g | Total Carbs: 17.5g | Protein: 2.9g.

CHICKPEA CHOCOLATE CHIP COOKIE DOUGH

Servings: 6 | Prep Time: 5 Minutes

INGREDIENTS

1 cup chickpeas, skins removed, patted dry

1/3 cup natural peanut butter

1-1/2 teaspoons vanilla extract

2 tablespoons agave nectar

1/3 cup vegan chocolate chips

This is a great healthy treat that dieters and kids will love. Though dough isn't for baking but is for eating as is. The dough contains a lot of fiber and protein thanks to the chickpeas.

DIRECTIONS

1. Remove the skins from the chickpeas, and pat them dry.

2. Put all of the ingredients EXCEPT for the chocolate chips in your food processor, and process on speed 2 until completely smooth.

3. Transfer the dough to a bowl, and using a wooden spoon mix in the chocolate chips.

Nutritional Info: Calories: 241 | Sodium: 76mg | Dietary Fiber: 6.9g | Total Fat: 10.1g | Total Carbs: 29.4g | Protein: 10.2g.

COCONUT CRACK BARS

Servings: 6-8 Bars | Prep Time: 10 Minutes

INGREDIENTS

cup shredded coconut, unsweetened

/4 cup maple syrup

tablespoons coconut oil

/2 teaspoon vanilla extract

/8 teaspoon salt

These no bake bars are sure to please any coconut lover, because they're brimming with coconut deliciousness. They're really easy to make, and take around 10 minutes to complete.

DIRECTIONS

1. Put all of the ingredients in your food processor, and process on speed 1 until well mixed.

2. Put the mixture in a 7x5 container. Place the container in the refrigerator for a minimum of an hour. Slice into bars after you take the container out of the refrigerator.

Nutritional Info: Calories: 91 | Sodium: 38mg | Dietary Fiber: 0.9g | Total Fat: 6.8g | Total Carbs: 8.1g | Protein: 0.3g.

FOIE GRAS POUTINE

Servings: 4 | Prep Time: 1 Minute | Cook Time: 7 Minutes

INGREDIENTS

FOIE GRAS SAUCE:

200 grams fresh foie gras

6 egg yolks

2-1/2 cups poutine sauce

1/4 cup 35% m.f. cream

FOIE GRAS AND PRESENTA:

4 slices fresh foie gras

14 ounces cheese curds

4 white-fleshed potatoes (cut into French fries)

Oil for frying

This is an incredibly indulgent snack that combines the decadent flavor of foie gras, the rich flavor of poutine (gravy), and everyone's favorite French fries. It's truly delicious, but not for those on a diet.

Nutritional Info: Calories: 887 | Sodium: 856mg | Dietary Fiber: 8.1g | Total Fat: 72.7g | Total Carbs: 84.9g | Protein: 30g.

DIRECTIONS

SAUCE:

1. Bring 2 cups of poutine to a boil in a saucepan.

2. Put the remaining ingredients in your food processor and process on speed 2 until smooth.

3. Add the poutine to the foie gras mixture SLOWLY.

4. Put the new mixture back in the pan, and heat on medium- low heat until the sauce reaches 175F, stir frequently throughout. You can attach a candy thermometer to the pan to check the temperature.

5. Once the sauce reaches 175F, take it off the heat, stirring frequently for another 30 seconds. Keep the sauce warm while making the rest of the dish.

FOIE GRAS AND PRESENTA:

6. Cut the potatoes into French fries. Make sure the foie gras slice are 1-inch thick, cut them down if necessary. Preheat the oven to 450F.

7. Sear the foie gras, in an extremely hot pan, until it turns brown. Once brown, put the slices on a baking sheet, and place in the oven for 4 to 5 minutes.

8. Put the cheese curd in a mound on whatever plates you're serving the dish in.

9. Fry the fries in the oil until they're golden brown, and crispy. Then put them on top of the cheese curds. Top the fries with a slice of foie gras. Then cover with the foie gras sauce. Dot with some of the unused plain poutine

10. Serve immediately.

NO BAKE VEGAN BROWNIES WITH GANACHE FROSTING

> Servings: 12 | Prep Time: 20 Minutes | Bake Time: 1 Minute

INGREDIENTS

BROWNIES:

1-1/2 cups raw walnuts

1 cup raw almonds

2-1/2 cups dates

3/4 cups cacao powder

2 tablespoons cacao nibs + more for topping

1/4 teaspoon sea salt

GANACHE FROSTING:

1/4 cup almond milk

1 cup dairy-free dark chocolate

2 tablespoons coconut oil

1/4 - 1/2 cup powdered sugar

1/4 teaspoon sea salt

These brownies are so decadent and delicious you won't even realize they're vegan. The ganache frosting gives the brownies an extra dimension of flavor.

Nutritional Info: Calories: 418 | Sodium: 91mg | Dietary Fiber: 9.8g | Total Fat: 24.2g | Total Carbs: 53.1g | Protein: 10.6g.

DIRECTIONS

1. Pit the dates and soak them in warm water for 10 minutes if they're dry. Chop the chocolate. Line an 8x8 dish with parchment paper. Roughly chop 1/2 cup walnuts.

2. Put 1 cup of almonds and walnuts in your food processor, and process on speed 1 until the nuts are ground finely.

3. Put in the sea salt and cacao powder, and pulse until all ingredients are combined. Put the mixture into a separate bowl.

4. Put the dates in your food processor, and process on speed 1 until the dates become small pieces. Transfer them to a small bowl.

5. Put the nut mixture back in the food processor, and start processing on speed one. Put the dates in, handfuls at a time while the machine is running until a dough is formed. Stop adding dates when you can grab a handful of the dough without it breaking apart in your hand.

6. Put the dough in the 8x8 dish. Put in roughly chopped walnuts and cacao nibs, and toss until all ingredients are well combined. Push the mixture down until it's completely flat in the dish.

7. Use the parchment paper to lift the brownies out of the dish. Gently squeeze in the sides to condense the brownies, making them thicker, and creating a smaller square.

8. Put the brownies back into the dish, and place in the refrigerator for 10 to 15 minutes. While the brownies are chilling, put the almond milk in a saucepan, and heat until just simmering. Put the warm almond milk in a mixing bowl.

9. Quickly put the chocolate in the bowl with the milk, and cover it loosely. Let the mixture rest undisturbed for 2 minutes.

10. While the mixture is sitting melt the coconut oil.

11. Mix in the sea salt, and coconut oil with the chocolate, almond milk mixture. Use a whisk when mixing in the coconut oil. Place the mixture in the refrigerator for 10 minutes.

12. After the 10 minutes, add powdered sugar in small doses to help make the frosting thicker. Use a whisk to mix. If it won't get thick enough add in a couple tablespoons of powdered sugar, and whisk again until the frosting is fluffy.

13. Add the frosting to the top of the brownies. If desired top with cacao nibs and/or walnuts. Slice the brownies into 12 pieces.

SOUTHWESTERN HASH BROWNS

Servings: 2 | Prep Time: 15 Minutes | Cook Time: 15-20 Minutes

INGREDIENTS

4 medium russet potatoes

1 red pepper

1 green pepper

1 jalapeno

2 cloves garlic

1/2 red pepper

1/4 cup cilantro

1/4 cup olive oil

Salt and pepper

1 avocado, sliced (garnish)

Hot sauce (garnish)

This is a delicious and easy way to add some flavor to your hash browns. The jalapeno gives it a nice kick, while the vegetables add a savory flavor.

DIRECTIONS

1. Dice the green and red peppers. Mince the garlic and cilantro. Peel the potato. Deseed and mince the jalapeno.

2. Using the disc attachment, grate the potatoes on speed 1.

3. Wash and thoroughly dry the grated potatoes.

4. Mix the veggies in a bowl EXCEPT for the potatoes. Once mixed, add the potatoes, and mix again. Salt and pepper to taste.

5. Place a healthy amount of olive oil on a griddle, then add the hash browns. Cook the hash brown on the griddle, on medium-high heat for 5 minutes without disturbing them.

6. They should start to brown at this point. Flip them over. Cook for a total of 15 to 20 minutes. Cut the hash browns into 2 servings.

7. Garnish with avocado, and serve with hot sauce.

Nutritional Info: Calories: 760 | Sodium: 38mg | Dietary Fiber: 20.0g | Total Fat: 45.6g | Total Carbs: 84.8g | Protein: 10.7g.

EGGLESS CHOCOLATE CHIP COOKIE DOUGH TRUFFLES

Servings: 18-20 truffles | Prep Time: 15 Minutes

INGREDIENTS

1/2 can chickpeas or white beans

1 teaspoon pure vanilla extract

Scant 1/8 teaspoon salt

Scant 1/8 teaspoon baking soda

2 tablespoons nut butter or oil

1/3 cup brown sugar

2 tablespoons chocolate chips

1-2 tablespoons quick oats

OPTIONAL:

1 bag chocolate chips

Milk of choice if needed, to thin it out

These delicious little treats use chickpeas as their base. You would never no though, and it makes these truffles healthy containing, no eggs, flour, or butter.

DIRECTIONS

1. Drain and rinse the chickpeas.

2. Place all the ingredients EXCEPT for the chocolate chips in your food processor. Process the ingredients on speed 1 until completely smooth.

3. Place the mixture on a bowl and mix in the chocolate chips. Form the mixture into small balls. You can use a melon baller for this.

4. If desired place the balls in the refrigerator for a while. While that's happening melt the bag of chocolate chips and 2 teaspoons of coconut oil.

5. Take the chilled truffles out of the refrigerator and coat them with the chocolate mixture. Put them back in the refrigerator to set the chocolate.

6. Serve once the chocolate is hard.

Nutritional Info: Calories: 10 | Sodium: 27mg | Dietary Fiber: 1.2g | Total Fat: 1.7g | Total Carbs: 6.8g | Protein: 1.4g.

LEMON BARS

Servings: 24 Bars | Prep Time: 15 Minutes | Bake Time: 1 Hour

INGREDIENTS

CRUST:

Vegetable oil for greasing

1-1/2 sticks unsalted butter, diced

2 cups all¬-purpose flour

1/4 cup light brown sugar

1/2 cup confectioner's sugar

1/4 teaspoon salt

FOR THE FILLING:

4 large eggs, plus 2 egg yolks

2 cups granulated sugar

1/3 cup all-purpose flour, sifted

1 teaspoon grated lemon zest 1 cup fresh

These are the lemon version of brownies. They're moist, and bursting with sweet lemon flavor.

DIRECTIONS

1. Preheat your oven to 350F. Dice the butter. Sift the 1/3 cup all-purpose flour for the filling. Use the vegetable oil to grease a 9x13 pan, then line it with aluminum foil, giving a 2-inch overhang from the sides. Grease the aluminum foil as well.

2. Put the remaining crust ingredients in your food processor, and pulse until the ingredients become a dough, around 1 minute.

3. Take the dough and press it into the pan, allowing it to come up about 1/2-inch on the sides of the pan. Bake the crust for 25 minutes on the middle rack. It should be golden brown when done.

4. While the crust is baking, use a whisk to combine the eggs, flour, and sugar until it becomes smooth. Then mix in the lemon juice, and zest using the whisk to mix.

5. Take the crust out of the oven when done. Lower the oven temperature to 300F. Pour the lemon mixture evenly onto the crust. Bake the bars for 30 to 35 minutes on the middle rack, until the filling has set.

6. Allow the bars to cool before refrigerating them for a minimum of 2 hours. Use the foil to take the bars out of the pan. Slice them into 24 pieces, sprinkle with confectioners' sugar, and serve.

Nutritional Info: Calories: 185 | Sodium: 76mg | Dietary Fiber: 0g | Total Fat: 6.7g | Total Carbs: 30.0g | Protein: 2.4g.

TUNA PATE

Servings: 6-8 | Prep Time: 15 Minutes

INGREDIENTS

2 (5-ounce) can packed in water tuna

1/2 cup onion, quartered

1 cup sliced almonds

1/2 teaspoon salt

1/4 teaspoon pepper

2 - 3 dashes tabasco sauce

1/2 cup butter

4 tablespoons sweet relish

3 tablespoons parsley

This is a great snack for game day or when having a party. Serve it with your favorite crackers.

DIRECTIONS

1. Drain and flake the tuna. Quarter the onion. Toast the almonds. Slice the butter into small chunks. Use plastic wrap to line the dish you're serving the pate in.

2. Put the almonds, onions, and tuna in your food processor. Pulse a few times.

3. Put in the tabasco, parsley, salt, pepper, and sliced butter. Pulse until all ingredients are well mixed. Put in the relish, and pulse again until the relish is incorporated.

4. Place the pate in the serving dish. Put it in the refrigerator, covered. Take the pate out 15 minutes before you intend on serving it.

5. Serve with your favorite crackers.

Nutritional Info: Calories: 250 | Sodium: 310mg | Dietary Fiber: 1.8g | Total Fat: 20.4g | Total Carbs: 6.0g | Protein: 12.2g.

VEGAN CASHEW CREAM CHEESE

Servings: 1 Cup | Prep Time: 5 Minutes + 4-8 Hours for soaking

INGREDIENTS

1 cup raw cashews

2 tablespoons nutritional yeast flakes

1/4 cup lemon juice

1/2 tablespoon canola oil

1/4 teaspoon salt

1 teaspoon apple cider vinegar

This vegan treat gets its creaminess from the cashews. Try adding in your favorite cream cheese flavors like scallions or onions.

DIRECTIONS

1. Soak the cashews for 4-8 hours.
2. Drain the cashews, and process them in your food processor on speed 2 until completely smooth.
3. Add in the remaining ingredients and process on speed 1 until all ingredients are well combined.
4. If you are adding in any flavors, mix them in, and serve.

Nutritional Info: Calories: 935 | Sodium: 628mg | Dietary Fiber: 9.4g | Total Fat: 72.1g | Total Carbs: 55.3g | Protein: 30.6g.

CHAPTER
11

SIDES

BROCCOLI AND QUINOA SALAD

Servings: 6 | Prep Time: 15 Minutes | Cook Time: 10 Minutes

INGREDIENTS

1 cup quinoa, uncooked

1-1/2 cups water + pinch of salt

1 cup slivered almonds

1-1/2 pounds broccoli

1 cup herbs

3 tablespoons extra virgin olive oil

1/2 lemon, zest

1/2 tablespoon lemon juice

3/4 teaspoons salt

1/4 teaspoon fresh ground pepper

This salad has a wonderful light flavor, that's enhanced by the lemon juice. The broccoli, quinoa, and almonds combine for a lovely crunchy texture.

DIRECTIONS

1. Cut the broccoli into large pieces. Finely chop the herbs.

2. Put the water, quinoa, and pinch of salt in a medium pan. Bring the mixture up to a boil, covered, then lower to low heat, and allow the quinoa to cook for 10 minutes. Once it's cooked, allow the quinoa to rest for 5 minutes, before using a fork to fluff it.

3. While the quinoa is cooking, heat a small skillet on low heat. Once hot, add the almonds, and cook until toasted. Stir the almonds a little while cooking.

4. Put the broccoli in your food processor in batches, and pulse until the broccoli is coarsely chopped.

5. Place all the ingredients in a large bowl, and mix until combined.

6. Allow the salad to cool before serving.

Nutritional Info: Calories: 309 | Sodium: 334mg | Dietary Fiber: 9.2g | Total Fat: 17.2g | Total Carbs: 32.7g | Protein: 11.4g.

CHEESE HERB CRISPS

Servings: 72 Crackers | Prep Time: 1 Hour 15 Minutes | Bake Time: 12 Minutes

INGREDIENTS

1-1/2 cups all-purpose flour

1/2 cup butter, softened

2 cups (8 ounces) shredded mozzarella cheese

1/4 cup (1 ounce) shredded parmesan cheese

1/2 teaspoon dried oregano

1/2 teaspoon salt

1/2 teaspoon freshly ground black pepper

3 tablespoons milk

2 teaspoons dried basil

2 tablespoons minced sun dried tomatoes

These are high end cheese crackers that you can easily make at home. Making them at home keeps preservatives and chemicals out of your crackers. These delicious crackers go great with Mediterranean food.

DIRECTIONS

1. Put the flour and butter in your food processor, and process on speed 1 until the ingredients are well mixed. Put the rest of the ingredients in your Hamilton Beach food processor, and process on speed 1 until well combined.

2. Put the mixture on wax paper or plastic wrap. Using the paper or wrap to help, create 1/4 to 1/2 logs out of the mixture. Twist the ends of the wrap or paper to seal, and refrigerate until firm, around 1 hour.

3. Preheat your oven to 350F.

4. Once firm, slice the logs into 1/8 inch pieces.

5. Transfer the pieces to a baking sheet. Bake the crisps for about 12 minutes. Flip the crisps after 6 minutes and continue to bake, until golden.

Nutritional Info: Calories: 31 | Sodium: 48mg | Dietary Fiber: 0g | Total Fat: 2.0g | Total Carbs: 2.2g | Protein: 1.3g.

CONFETTI SALAD

Servings: 10 | Prep Time: 1 Hour 15 Minutes

INGREDIENTS

4 cups cauliflower

4 cups broccoli

2 cups carrot

2 cups celery

1 red pepper

1 cup onion

2 garlic cloves

1/4 cup apple cider vinegar

3 tablespoons good olive oil

2 teaspoons Italian seasoning

1 teaspoon kosher salt

1/4 teaspoon fresh ground black pepper

This a beautiful multicolored salad, that's perfect to bring to any event. It's very light, tasty, and packed with nutrition.

DIRECTIONS

1. Roughly chop the cauliflower, broccoli, carrots, celery, red pepper, and onion. Mince the garlic.

2. Put the carrots in your food processor, and pulse until the carrots are finely chopped. Transfer the carrots to a big bowl.

3. Repeat the process with the rest of the vegetables.

4. Use a whisk to mix the garlic and vinegar. Then add in the oil, Italian seasoning, salt and pepper, and whisk again.

5. Toss the dressing with the vegetables in the big bowl.

6. Refrigerate for at least an hour before serving.

Nutritional Info: Calories: 84 | Sodium: 290mg | Dietary Fiber: 3.3g | Total Fat: 4.7g | Total Carbs: 9.5g | Protein: 2.4g.

CREOLE SEAFOOD SEASONING

Servings: 2 Cups | Prep Time: 2 Minutes

INGREDIENTS

/3 cup sea salt

/4 cup garlic powder

/4 cup black pepper

tablespoons cayenne pepper

tablespoons dried thyme

tablespoons dried basil

tablespoons dried oregano

/3 cup paprika

tablespoons onion powder

This seasoning has all the flavor you expect to find in New Orleans. Making this mixture at home allows you to make a large amount to keep on hand, and saves you lots of money compared to store bought seasoning.

DIRECTIONS

1. Place all the ingredients in your food processor, and pulse until the ingredients are well combined.

2. Store the seasoning in an airtight container.

Nutritional Info: Calories: 8 | Sodium: 1mg | Dietary Fiber: 0.8g | Total Fat: 0.3g | Total Carbs: 1.7g | Protein: 0.4g.

HASHED BRUSSEL SPROUTS WITH LEMON

> Servings: 4-6 | Prep Time: 15 Minutes | Cook Time: 10 Minutes

INGREDIENTS

2 tablespoons lemon juice

1 lemon, zest

2 to 3 pounds brussels sprouts

2 tablespoons olive oil

2 tablespoons butter

3 garlic cloves, minced

2 tablespoons mustard seeds

1/4 cup dry white wine

Salt and pepper to taste

These Brussel sprouts have a deliciously light flavor thanks to the lemon. They're a great side dish for a nice piece of fish or chicken.

DIRECTIONS

1. Mince the garlic. Cut the bottoms off of the Brussel sprouts. Put the lemon juice in a big bowl and set aside.

2. Put batches of the Brussel sprouts in your food process, and process on speed 1 until the sprouts are thinly sliced.

3. Transfer the finished sprouts to the bowl with the lemon juice. Toss the sprouts with the juice when finished processing.

4. In a large skillet heat the oil and butter on high heat. Put in the mustard seeds, garlic, and Brussel sprouts, stir frequently.

5. Cook for around 4 minutes, until the Brussel sprouts, are wilted. The sprouts should still be green in color.

6. Put in the wine, and salt and pepper to taste. Stir, while cooking for another minute. Take the skillet off the heat and add more salt, pepper and lemon juice if necessary.

7. Mix in the majority of lemon zest.

8. Serve with a garnish of lemon zest.

Nutritional Info: Calories: 202 | Sodium: 86mg | Dietary Fiber: 9.2g | Total Fat: 10.4g | Total Carbs: 23.0g | Protein: 8.9g.

KALE AND BRUSSEL SPROUTS SALAD

Servings: 8 | Prep Time: 20 Minutes

INGREDIENTS

3 cups brussels sprouts

1 large bunch Tuscan kale

1 small clove garlic

1 small shallot

1 cup finely grated pecorino

1/2 cup extra virgin olive oil

1/2 cup toasted pine nuts

2 tablespoons Dijon mustard

3 lemons

Salt and freshly ground black pepper

This easy to make salad has a delicious citrus flavor. The citrus cuts the bitterness of the Brussel sprouts and kale. If the dressing is too tart, try adding a teaspoon of sugar.

DIRECTIONS

1. Zest and juice the lemons. Remove the center stem from the kale.

2. Place the kale in your food processor, and process it on speed 1 until it's shredded.

3. Set kale aside, and repeat the process with the Brussel sprouts. Then put in the shallots and garlic, and process on speed 1 until the garlic is minced, and the shallots are shredded.

4. Whisk the rest of the ingredients in a big bowl to combine them. Then put in the vegetables, and toss to coat the vegetables.

5. Let the salad sit for 10 minutes before serving.

Nutritional Info: Calories: 209 | Sodium: 18mg | Dietary Fiber: 2.7g | Total Fat: 19.4g | Total Carbs: 9.1g | Protein: 3.8g.

PARMESAN SPINACH CAKES

Servings: 4 | Prep Time: 15 Minutes | Cook Time: 20 Minutes

INGREDIENTS

12 ounces fresh spinach

1/2 cup part-skim ricotta cheese

1/2 cup finely shredded Parmesan cheese

2 large eggs

1 clove garlic, minced

1/4 teaspoon salt

1/4 teaspoon freshly ground pepper

These cakes are just like little spinach, and cheese pies. The parmesan gives a nice salty flavor to the spinach.

DIRECTIONS

1. Mince the garlic. Preheat your oven to 400F. Beat the eggs. Grease a muffin tin with cooking spray.

2. Place the spinach in your food processor in batches, and pulse until it's finely chopped. Place the spinach in a bowl.

3. Place the rest of the ingredients in the bowl with the spinach and mix until well combined.

4. Put the mixture in the muffin tin.

5. Allow the cakes to bake for around 20 minutes, until the cakes set. Allow the cakes to rest 5 minutes before removing from the tin.

6. Serve the cakes while they're still warm, and garnish with more parmesan if desired.

Nutritional Info: Calories: 194 | Sodium: 562mg | Dietary Fiber: 1.9g | Total Fat: 11.6g | Total Carbs: 6.3g | Protein: 18.7g.

PKHALI

Servings: 4-6 | Prep Time: 13 Minutes | Cook Time: 1 Minutes

INGREDIENTS

-1/2 pounds baby spinach

-1/2 cups toasted walnuts

/2 cup cilantro

/2 cup parsley

teaspoon hot paprika

/2 teaspoon ground turmeric

/2 teaspoon ground fenugreek

3 tablespoons olive oil

2 tablespoons red wine vinegar

2 cloves garlic

1 small yellow onion

Pomegranate seeds, for garnish

Kosher salt and freshly ground black pepper, to taste

Pkhali is a lovely spinach and walnut salad. All the ingredients a pureed and get a nice sweetness from the pomegranate seeds that it's topped with.

DIRECTIONS

1. Chop the cilantro and parsley. Roughly chop the garlic and onion. Put ice water into a bowl.

2. In a large pot, place salted water, and bring it to a bowl. Once boiling, put in the spinach, cook for about 1 minute, until the spinach wilts. Once wilted, put the spinach into the bowl of ice water.

3. Drain the spinach and remove as much water as possible by squeezing the spinach.

4. Put the spinach in your food processor, and process on speed 1 until almost smooth. Place the smooth spinach in a bowl and set aside.

5. Put the remaining ingredients EXCEPT for the pomegranate seeds in your food processor, and process on speed 2 until smooth.

6. Mix the 2 purees together, and serve, garnished with pomegranate seeds.

Nutritional Info: Calories: 294 | Sodium: 95mg | Dietary Fiber: 5.5g | Total Fat: 26.1g | Total Carbs: 10.2g | Protein: 11.3g.

PLANTAIN HUSH PUPPIES

Servings: 4 | Prep Time: 25 Minutes | Cook Time: 20 Minutes

INGREDIENTS

3 cloves garlic, finely chopped

Juice of 1 orange (about 1/3 cup)

4 teaspoons fresh lime juice

1 tablespoon extra-virgin olive oil

Salt

2 avocados

Vegetable oil, for frying

2 ripe plantains, peeled and quartered

1 (16-ounce) bag frozen corn, thawed

1-1/2 teaspoons baking powder

Hush puppies are small savory fried dough balls that a traditionally served with seafood. This variation has a sweetness thanks to the plantains.

DIRECTIONS

1. Finely chop the garlic, and thaw the corn. Peel and quarter the plantain. Use paper towels to line a baking sheet.

2. Mix 1 teaspoon lime juice, garlic and orange juice, then use a whisk to add in the olive oil, and salt to taste. Set aside for later.

3. Place the avocados, and lime juice in your Hamilton Beach food processor, and process on speed 2 until pureed. Salt to taste. Transfer to a bowl, and set aside.

4. Put the plantains and 1-1/2 cups of corn in your food processor. Process on speed 2 until pureed. Place in a bowl, and mix in 1 teaspoon of salt, and the baking powder.

5. Pour enough oil into a large pot to fill it up to a depth of 3 inches. Heat the oil to 335F. Use a candy thermometer to check the oil temperature.

6. Drop large tablespoons of the plantain mixture into the hot oil in batches of 6. Fry for about 3 minutes, until the batter puffs up, and turns golden brown.

7. Place the finished hush puppies on the baking sheet to drain. Salt to taste. Let the oil reheat to 335F between batches.

8. Serve the hush puppies while still hot with the avocado, and orange dipping sauces.

Nutritional Info: Calories: 449 | Sodium: 13mg | Dietary Fiber: 11.6g | Total Fat: 24.2g | Total Carbs: 62.7g | Protein: 6.2g.

SHRIMP COBB SALAD

Servings: 2 | Prep Time: 30 Minutes | Cook Time: 1 Hour 40 Minutes

INGREDIENTS

1 pound medium shrimp

2 tablespoons olive oil, divided

1 tablespoon creole seasoning

4 slices bacon

2 large eggs

5 cups romaine lettuce

1 avocado

1 cup canned corn kernels

1/2 cup crumbled goat cheese

FOR THE CILANTRO LIME VINAIGRETTE:

1 cup loosely packed cilantro

Juice of 1 lime

1 jalapeño, optional

2 cloves garlic

Kosher salt and freshly ground black pepper, to taste

2 tablespoons olive oil

2 tablespoons apple cider vinegar

This salad is nice and light, but still full of flavor. The shrimp, avocado, and bacon combine for a wonderful variety of textures.

DIRECTIONS

1. Preheat your oven to 400F. Peel and devein the shrimp. Dice the bacon. Peel, deseed, and chop the avocado. Drain the corn. Remove the stems from the cilantro. Use parchment paper to line a baking sheet. Line a plate with paper towels.

2. Place the lime juice, garlic, jalapeno, and cilantro in your food processor. Start processing on speed 1 and slowly pour in both the oil and vinegar in. Keep processing until the dressing emulsifies.

3. Put the shrimp on the lined baking sheet, and combine with the oil and creole seasoning. Cook in the oven for 4 to 5 minutes. The shrimp should be cooked through, and pink.

4. Put the bacon in a skillet that's been heated on medium-high heat. Cook the bacon for 6 to 8 minutes, until it gets crispy and turns brown. Place the bacon on the paper towel lined plate to drain.

5. In a large pot place the eggs and enough cold water to cover the eggs by an inch. Bring the eggs to a boil. Once boiling, allow to eggs to cook for 1 minute.

6. Take the pot off the heat, and cover it. Let the pot sit for 8 to 10 minutes. Then drain the eggs and allow them to cool before you peel them, and dice them.

7. In a large bowl, put the romaine. Then put in the remaining ingredients, and drizzle in the dressing.

8. Serve immediately.

Nutritional Info: Calories: 1251 | Sodium: 3108mg | Dietary Fiber: 10.0g | Total Fat: 89.4g | Total Carbs: 32.1g | Protein: 88.7g.

SWEET AND SPICE COLESLAW

Servings: 6-8 | Prep Time: 2 Hours 30 Minutes | Cook Time:

INGREDIENTS

pounds green cabbage

carrots

medium yellow onion

/2 cup mayonnaise

/4 cup mustard

teaspoons apple cider vinegar

cup sugar

teaspoon black pepper

1/2 teaspoon cayenne

Salt and freshly ground black pepper to taste

This coleslaw gets a nice bit of heat from the cayenne, but has a sweet flavor thanks to the sugar. Serve it as a side with fried chicken, or on top of a pork sandwich.

DIRECTIONS

1. Peel the carrots and if necessary cut them into small enough pieces to fit in the chute of your food processor. Do the same thing with the onion Cut the cabbage into quarters, and remove the core.

2. Use the disk attachment with the grater side up to grate the vegetables on speed 1. Transfer the vegetable to a bowl and mix them together.

3. Whisk together the remaining ingredients EXCEPT for the salt and pepper to taste. Combine the mixture with the vegetable and salt and pepper to taste.

4. Cover and refrigerate for at least 2 hours before serving.

Nutritional Info: Calories: 222 | Sodium: 147mg | Dietary Fiber: 4.7g | Total Fat: 6.5g | Total Carbs: 41.3g | Protein: 3.2g.

SPRING PEA AND RICOTTA CROSTINI

Servings: 25-30 Crostini | Prep Time: 10 Minutes | Bake Time: 8 Minutes

INGREDIENTS

FOR CROSTINI:

1 baguette

Extra virgin olive oil

Kosher salt

FOR PEA PURÉE:

1 cup frozen sweet peas

1/2 cup fresh ricotta cheese

1/2 cup fresh parmesan cheese

1 tablespoon extra-virgin olive oil

1 tablespoon lemon juice

1/4 teaspoon lemon zest

1/2 clove garlic

3-4 basil leaves

1/2 teaspoon salt

Freshly ground black pepper

Parmesan cheese, basil and extra virgin olive oil (garnish)

This is the perfect side dish for spring. The peas and ricott are creamy and sweet. The create the perfect contrast to the saltiness of the parmesan.

DIRECTIONS

1. Thaw the peas. Grate the parmesan. Mince the garlic, and chop the basil. Preheat your oven to 400F.

2. Slice the bread, coat with olive oil, and salt to taste. Bake until the edges become slightly golden, 6-8 minutes.

3. Wash the peas and gently dry them.

4. Put all of the remaining ingredients, including salt and pepper in your food processor. Pulse the ingredients until the mixture is almost smooth.

5. Cover one side of the crostini with a nice layer of the pea mixture. Garnish with parmesan, basil, and a little olive oil.

Nutritional Info: Calories: 49 | Sodium: 130.5mg | Dietary Fiber: 0.3g | Total Fat: 1.7g | Total Carbs: 5.1g | Protein: 2.6g.

WHITE BEAN PUREE

Servings: 4 | Prep Time: 5 Minutes | Cook Time: 5 Minutes

INGREDIENTS

2 teaspoons olive oil

3 garlic cloves, minced

2 cans white beans, drained and rinsed

2 tablespoons lemon juice

1/2 teaspoon salt

This dish has a creamy texture, and a light nutty flavor. Try serving it in place of mashed potatoes with your next meal.

DIRECTIONS

1. Drain and rinse the white beans. Mince the garlic.

2. Heat the oil in a saucepan on medium-high heat. Put in the garlic, stirring until it becomes flagrant, around 30 seconds. Add in the beans and 1/4 cup of water.

3. Simmer the ingredients for about 4 minutes, until the beans are heated through.

4. Allow the beans to cool a little. Then put them in your food processor, add the lemon juice and salt, and pulse until the beans are mostly pureed. They shouldn't be completely smooth.

5. Serve warm.

Nutritional Info: Calories: 475 | Sodium: 314mg | Dietary Fiber: 20.6g | Total Fat: 3.5g | Total Carbs: 82.3g | Protein: 31.7g.

CHAPTER
12

DIPS AND SAUCES

BLACK BEAN HUMMUS

Servings: 8 | Prep Time: 5 Minutes

INGREDIENTS

1 clove garlic

1 (15 ounce) can black beans

2 tablespoons lemon juice

1-1/2 tablespoons tahini

3/4 teaspoons ground cumin

1/2 teaspoon salt

1/4 teaspoon cayenne pepper

1/4 teaspoon paprika

10 greek olives

This hummus variation on hummus has a deeper flavor thanks to the black beans. It goes great with pita chips, and pieces of toasted pita.

DIRECTIONS

1. Drain the black beans, and keep the liquid.

2. Put the garlic in your food processor, and process on speed 1 until minced. Put in 1/8 teaspoon cayenne, the black beans, lemon juice, 1/2 teaspoon cumin, 1/2 teaspoon, and tahini. And process on speed 2 until completely smooth. Taste the hummus.

3. Season to taste with remaining seasoning, extra bean liquid, and lemon juice to taste.

4. Serve with a garnish of olives.

Nutritional Info: Calories: 207 | Sodium: 202mg | Dietary Fiber: 8.6g | Total Fat: 2.9g | Total Carbs: 34.5g | Protein: 12.1g.

BUTTER

Servings: 3/4 cups / 12 Tablespoons | Prep Time: 10 Minutes

INGREDIENTS

1 pint heavy cream

Pinch of sea salt or kosher salt

You can easily make butter at home in just 10 minutes. Making butter at home allows you to use organic ingredients to make butter at a fraction of the price.

DIRECTIONS

1. Place the heavy cream in your food processor and process on speed 1 for around 6 to 7 minutes. After about 3 minutes use a spatula to scrape the bits off the sides of the bowl.

2. Put the butter in a strainer and use cold water to gently wash it. Then strain the butter.

3. Add the salt, and knead it into the butter using your hands until it gets creamy.

4. Serve immediately or store in an airtight container for 2 weeks.

Nutritional Info: Calories: 138 | Sodium: 35mg | Dietary Fiber: 0.0g | Total Fat: 14.8g | Total Carbs: 1.1g | Protein: 0.8g.

CASHEW DILL DIP

Servings: 1/2 cup | Prep Time: Overnight soaking + 5 Minutes

INGREDIENTS

1/2 cup of cashews

1-2 tablespoons of lemon juice

Pinch of salt

1-2 tablespoons fresh dill leaves

This dip is so creamy from the dill, but contains no dairy. It's a great dip for vegetables. Try it at your next party.

DIRECTIONS

1. Soak the cashews overnight. If you're in a pinch soak them for 30 minutes in hot water.

2. Place all the ingredients in your food processor and process on speed 2 until the dip is smooth.

3. Serve with your favorite vegetables.

Nutritional Info: Calories: 416 | Sodium: 185mg | Dietary Fiber: 3.0g | Total Fat: 32.3g | Total Carbs: 26.5g | Protein: 12.0g.

GREEN GODDESS DIP

Servings: 1-1/2 Cups | Prep Time: 10 Minutes

INGREDIENTS

avocado

anchovy fillets

small garlic cloves

scallions

/4 cup white wine vinegar

1-1/2 tablespoons lemon juice

1/4 cup Greek yogurt

1/4 cup basil

1 tablespoon fresh parsley

1 tablespoon tarragon leaves

At least 1/4 cup extra virgin olive oil, for making dressing, optional

This creamy dip does double duty as it can also be a dressing. It has a beautiful vibrant green flavor, and this version is healthier replacing the sour cream, and mayonnaise with avocado, and Greek yogurt.

DIRECTIONS

1. Chop the avocado, garlic, scallions, basil, parsley, and tarragon.

2. Place all the ingredients EXCEPT for the tarragon, basil, and parsley in your food processor, and process on speed 1 until mostly smooth.

3. Put in the remaining ingredients and process on speed 2 until completely smooth. If too thick add a little olive oil and process on speed one until combined

4. If you're making dressing add olive oil 1/4 cup at a time processing on speed 1 until desired consistency is reached.

5. Serve the dip with raw vegetables or chips. Use the dressing for salad or as a marinade for chicken.

Nutritional Info: Calories: 40 | Sodium: 30mg | Dietary Fiber: 0g | Total Fat: 4.1g | Total Carbs: 1.2g | Protein: 1.2g.

KALE WALNUT PESTO

Servings: 8 | Prep Time: 8 Minutes

INGREDIENTS

2 cups kale leaves

1 cup basil leaves

1 teaspoon sea salt

1/4 cup olive oil

1/4 cup walnuts, toasted

4 cloves garlic, chopped

1/2 cup grated cheese

This pesto alternative is bounding with nutrition. Both kale and walnuts provide ALA which is an Omega 3 Fatty Acid that helps protect brain cells. Kale is a superfood that is high in antioxidants.

DIRECTIONS

1. Remove the stems from the kale.

2. Place the kale, salt, and basil in your food processor, and pulse until the kale is well chopped. Turn the machine to speed 1, and slowly pour in the olive oil. Once the oil has been incorporated, scrape the bits off the sides of the bowl.

3. Put in the garlic and walnuts, and process on speed 1 until well incorporated. Put in the cheese, and pulse until well mixed.

4. Serve immediately with pasta, as a spread for sandwiches, or as a marinade for chicken.

Nutritional Info: Calories: 129 | Sodium: 357mg | Dietary Fiber: 0.6g | Total Fat: 11.3g | Total Carbs: 3.2g | Protein: 5.6g.

MISO TOFU RANCH

Servings: 2 Cups | Prep Time: 5 Minutes

INGREDIENTS

4 ounces tofu

3 tablespoons white miso

1 tablespoon lemon juice

2 teaspoons white wine vinegar

1/2 teaspoons garlic powder

1/2 teaspoons onion powder

1/4 teaspoons black pepper

1/2 cup sour cream

2 tablespoons fresh chives

1 tablespoon parsley

Raw vegetables

This ranch has more over a savory flavor thanks to the miso. The tofu makes this dip extra creamy.

DIRECTIONS

1. Drain the tofu. Chop the chives, and parsley.

2. Put the first 7 ingredients in your food processor, and process on speed 2 until pureed.

3. Place the mixture in a bowl, and combine with the sour cream, parsley, and chives.

4. Garnish the dip with more chives if desired, and serve with raw vegetables.

Nutritional Info: Calories: 224 | Sodium: 1002mg | Dietary Fiber: 2.2g | Total Fat: 16.1g | Total Carbs: 11.9g | Protein: 9.9g.

PESTO

Servings: 1 Cups | Prep Time: 15 Minutes

INGREDIENTS

2 cups fresh Basil leaves, packed

1/2 cup grated Romano or Parmigiano-Reggiano cheese

1/2 cup extra virgin olive oil

1/3 cup pine nuts

3 garlic cloves

Salt and pepper to taste

This traditional Italian sauce gets its flavor from the aromatic basil plant. You can choose to use either parmesan or Romano cheese. The Romano has a stronger flavor.

DIRECTIONS

1. Mince the garlic.

2. Put the basil and pine nuts in your food processor, and pulse until roughly chopped. Put in the garlic and cheese, and pulse a few more times, until ingredients are combined.

3. Put your food processor on speed 1 and drizzle in the olive oil, and keep the machine running until the sauce emulsifies. Salt and pepper to taste.

4. Use the sauce for pasta, sandwiches, or as a spread from bread.

Nutritional Info: Calories: 1573 | Sodium: 1100mg | Dietary Fiber: 2.6g | Total Fat: 157.4g | Total Carbs: 14.4g | Protein: 46.2g.

ROASTED BEET HUMMUS

Servings: 6 | Prep Time: 10 Minutes

INGREDIENTS

1 small roasted beet

1 (15-ounce) can chickpeas, cooked

Zest of one large lemon

Juice of half a large lemon

Pinch salt and black pepper

2 large cloves garlic, minced

2 heaping Tablespoon tahini

1/4 cup extra virgin olive oil

This hummus has a nice earthy flavor from the beets with a little citrus hint. It has a lovely pink flavor.

DIRECTIONS

1. Drain most of the liquid from the chickpeas.

2. Peel the beet, and put it in your food processor. Process on speed 1 until it's finely chopped.

3. Put in the rest of the ingredients EXCEPT for the olive oil. Process on speed 1 until the mixture becomes smooth.

4. With the machine still running slowly pour in the olive oil. Process until emulsified.

5. Salt and pepper to taste, and add more lemon juice if desired. Add a small amount of water if the hummus is too thick for your looking.

6. Serve immediately.

Nutritional Info: Calories: 370 | Sodium: 35mg | Dietary Fiber: 13.2g | Total Fat: 15.5g | Total Carbs: 46.4g | Protein: 14.9g.

ROASTED GARLIC BABAGANOUSH

Servings: 2-1/2 Cups | Prep Time: 10 Minutes | Cook Time: 60 Minutes

INGREDIENTS

1 large eggplant

1 head garlic

2 tablespoons olive oil

1 tablespoon coarse salt

1-2 tablespoons fresh lemon juice, to taste

Babaganoush is a dip made with eggplant, olive oil, and lemon juice. It is a Mediterranean favorite, and is a perfect dip for summertime.

DIRECTIONS

1. Preheat your oven to 350F. Peel the outer layers off the head of garlic and cut off the top. Use parchment paper to line a baking sheet. Rinse the eggplant, cut the ends off, and cut the eggplant in half lengthwise.

2. Put the eggplant, cut side down on the baking sheet. Make sure the halves are at least 1 inch apart. Place the garlic cut side up on the baking sheet as well. Bake until the eggplant becomes soft, around 60 minutes.

3. Let the eggplant cool a little. Slice the eggplant halves into 6 pieces.

4. Put the eggplants in your food processor, and pulse until roughly chopped. Then add in the remaining ingredients. Make sure to take the garlic cloves out of the husk before adding. Process on speed 1 until the mixture becomes smooth. The dip can be a little chunky if you prefer.

5. Serve once you are done processing.

Nutritional Info: Calories: 151 | Sodium: 7mg | Dietary Fiber: 6.5g | Total Fat: 11.6g | Total Carbs: 12.4g | Protein: 2.2g.

ROASTED SALSA VERDE

Servings: 2-1/2 Cups | Prep Time: 10 Minutes | Cook Time: 10 Minutes

INGREDIENTS

1-1/2 pounds tomatillos

1 to 2 medium jalapeños

1/2 cup white onion

1/4 cup packed fresh cilantro leaves

1 to 2 medium limes, juiced

1/2 to 1 teaspoon salt, to taste

Optional variation: 1 to 2 avocados

This salsa is made with roasted tomatillos and not tomatoes. Tomatillos look like green tomatoes, but are actual just members of the same vegetable family. Tomatillos have a tart flavor that gets mellowed out with the roasting. You can also add avocado to make this salsa creamy.

DIRECTIONS

1. Preheat your broil and place a rack around 4 inches from the broiler. Husk and rinse the tomatillos. Remove the stems from the jalapenos. Chop the onion. Dice the avocado if using.

2. Put the jalapenos and tomatillos on a baking sheet, and roast for around 5 minutes. The vegetable should have black spots when done. Turn the vegetables over, and roast for 4 to 6 minutes more. There should be more black spots, and blistering should occur.

3. While the tomatillos are roasting, place the remaining ingredients in your food processor EXCEPT for the avocado (if you're using it).

4. Add in the remaining ingredients once roasted. Pulse until the salsa is almost completely smooth. Add extras salt and lime juice if desired.

5. If you're using the avocados wait for the salsa to cool down, and then add in the avocados and pulse until smooth.

6. Serve salsa room temperature or chilled.

Nutritional Info: Calories: 333 | Sodium: 942mg | Dietary Fiber: 19.7g | Total Fat: 10.2g | Total Carbs: 61.8g | Protein: 10.0g.

SALSA

Servings: 20 | Prep Time: 10 Minutes

INGREDIENTS

3 cups tomatoes

1/2 cup green bell pepper

1 cup onion, diced

1/4 cup fresh cilantro

2 tablespoons fresh lime juice

4 teaspoons fresh jalapeno pepper

1/2 teaspoon ground cumin

1/2 teaspoon kosher salt

1/2 teaspoon ground black pepper

This classic Mexican dip is perfect with chips, or as a topping for tacos. The addition of cumin gives this salsa a full flavor.

DIRECTIONS

1. Roughly chop the tomatoes, bell pepper, onions, and jalapeno.

2. Place all the ingredients in your food processor, and pulse until ingredients are well combined, and desired consistency is reached.

3. Serve immediately or, chill in the refrigerator.

Nutritional Info: Calories: 9 | Sodium: 60mg | Dietary Fiber: 0.5g | Total Fat: 0.1g | Total Carbs: 1.9g | Protein: 0.4g.

SMOKED SALMON DIP

Servings: 2 Cups | Prep Time: 5 Minutes

INGREDIENTS

cup cream cheese

/4 cup sour cream

/4 cup mayonnaise

tablespoon fresh lemon juice

2 tablespoons capers

/4 teaspoon tabasco

4 ounces smoked salmon

2 tablespoons fresh dill

2 tablespoons fresh chives

Salt, to taste

This easy to make dip is very versatile. It's great for parties with cracker, or spread on bagels for breakfast or brunch.

DIRECTIONS

1. Roughly chop the salmon. Drain the capers. Chop the dill and chives.

2. Put the cream cheese, mayonnaise, sour cream, capers, tabasco, and lemon juice in your food processor and pulse until the ingredients are well combined. Add in the remaining ingredients, and pulse again until the salmon is finely chopped.

3. The dip can be refrigerated if necessary, but will become firm. Allow the dip to sit out for a bit before serving if refrigerated.

Nutritional Info: Calories: 651 | Sodium: 1961mg | Dietary Fiber: 0.8g | Total Fat: 58.1g | Total Carbs: 0.8g | Protein: 21.1g.

SPICY CHIPOTLE WHITE BEAN DIP

Servings: 4 | Prep Time: 5 Minutes

INGREDIENTS

1 (15-ounce) can cannellini beans

1-3 chipotle peppers in adobo sauce

2 cloves garlic

2 tablespoons lemon juice

1 teaspoon cumin

1 teaspoon chili powder

1/4 cup plus 2 tablespoons olive oil

This creamy dip gets a little heat, and a nice smoky flavor from the chipotles. A chipotle is a smoke dried, ripe jalapeno.

DIRECTIONS

1. Drain and rinse the cannellini beans.

2. Place all the ingredients EXCEPT for the olive oil in your food processor. Start processing on speed 1, and slowly add in the olive oil while the machine is running. Once you've started pouring in the oil turn the speed up to speed 2.

3. Process until the dip becomes emulsified.

4. Serve with chips or your favorite vegetables.

Nutritional Info: Calories: 484 | Sodium: 37mg | Dietary Fiber: 27.3g | Total Fat: 13.8g | Total Carbs: 68.2g | Protein: 26.1g.

SPINACH ARTICHOKE DIP

Servings: 8 | Prep Time: 20 Minutes

INGREDIENTS

14 ounces artichoke hearts in water

4 ounces cream cheese

1/4 cup plus 1 tablespoon grated Parmesan

1 tablespoon lemon juice

1 small garlic clove

1/8 teaspoon cayenne pepper

2 scallions

10 ounces chopped spinach

This classic dip is full of flavor thanks to the spinach, artichoke, and cheese. This version isn't quite as heavy because of the reduced fat cheese.

DIRECTIONS

1. Drain, rinse, and chop the artichoke. Thaw the spinach and squeeze it dry. Slice the scallions, and chop the garlic.

2. Put the cream cheese, 3 tablespoons of water, lemon juice, garlic half of the artichoke, 1/4 cup of parmesan, and cayenne in your food processor, and process on speed 1 until the mixture becomes smooth. Put in the remaining ingredients and pulse until the ingredients combine but are still chunky.

3. Serve immediately topped with the 1 tablespoon of parmesan.

Nutritional Info: Calories: 107 | Sodium: 186mg | Dietary Fiber: 3.6g | Total Fat: 6.8g | Total Carbs: 7.5g | Protein: 6.2g.

THAI PEANUT HUMMUS

Servings: 12 | Prep Time: 15 Minutes | Cook Time: 5 Minutes

INGREDIENTS

1/4 cup coconut oil

2 large cloves garlic

2 cups cooked garbanzo beans

1/4 cup fresh lime juice

1/4 cup peanut butter

1/4 cup coconut milk

1/4 cup sweet chili sauce

1/4 cup lemon grass

1/4 cup fresh Thai basil leaves

1 tablespoon fresh ginger

2 teaspoons green curry paste

1 jalapeno pepper

1/2 teaspoon salt

1 pinch cayenne pepper (optional)

1 pinch chili powder (optional)

This is not your traditional hummus. It has the perfect mix of flavor of Thai peanut sauce, and the rich creaminess of hummus.

DIRECTIONS

1. Mince the basil, lemon grass, and jalapeno. Use gloves when handling the jalapeno, and be carefully not to touch your eyes. Peel and grate the ginger. Thinly slice the garlic.

2. In a skillet, melt the coconut oil on medium heat. Once the oil is hot, put in the garlic and cook for about 30 seconds to a minute. The garlic should start to brown and be fragrant when ready. Allow the mixture to cool for a short time.

3. Place all the ingredients in your food processor on speed 2 until completely smooth.

4. Garnish with little pieces of peanut and a jalapeno slice if desired, and serve.

Nutritional Info: Calories: 222 | Sodium: 204mg | Dietary Fiber: 6.4g | Total Fat: 10.7g | Total Carbs: 25.2g | Protein: 8.1g.

WATERCRESS WALNUT DIP

Servings: 1-1/4 Cups | Prep Time: 5 Minutes

INGREDIENTS

2 ounces watercress

-1/2 teaspoons Dijon mustard

teaspoons lemon juice

tablespoon shallot

medium garlic cloves

tablespoons walnut oil

tablespoons olive oil

Kosher salt

This dip has a similar flavor to pesto. It has a pepper flavor from the watercress, and a nice nuttiness from the walnuts.

DIRECTIONS

1. Peel the garlic, and finely chop the shallots. Wash, remove the tough stems from the watercress, and dry it.

2. Put all the ingredients EXCEPT for the oils into your food processor, and pulse until well combined. Turn the machine to speed 1, and slowly pour in the oils, and continue processing until a thick sauce is formed. Salt to taste.

3. Refrigerate, covered, until time to serve.

Nutritional Info: Calories: 993 | Sodium: 181mg | Dietary Fiber: 8.5g | Total Fat: 98.2g | Total Carbs: 16.1g | Protein: 22.8g.

WHIPPED FETA WITH SWEET AND HOT PEPPERS

Servings: 2 Cups | Prep Time: 15 Minutes | Cook Time: 55 Minutes

INGREDIENTS

2 medium red bell peppers

1 pound feta cheese

2 teaspoons chili flakes

1 teaspoon crushed Urfa chili, plus a pinch for garnish

1/2 teaspoon Spanish paprika

1 teaspoon freshly squeezed lemon juice

1/4 cup olive oil

This creamy dip has a smoky and slightly flavor. It goes we with crackers and raw vegetables.

DIRECTIONS

1. Remove the stems, seeds, and white pith from the bell peppers, and cut them in half lengthwise. Drain and break the feta in 1/2-inch pieces. Preheat the broiler and position the rack in middle.

2. Put the peppers cut side down on a baking sheet and place in the broiler. Cook the peppers for about 15 minutes, until blackened, turning them throughout.

3. Put the peppers in a bowl, and cover with plastic wrap. Allow the peppers to rest until they are cool enough to touch. Once cooled, remove the peppers, and any liquid Peel and chop the peppers, and place them back in the bowl. Combine all the ingredients in the bowl.

4. Place the mixture in your food processor, and process on speed 2 until smooth.

5. Transfer the mixture to the refrigerator to set for 30 minutes.

6. Serve with a pinch of paprika, aleppo peppers, and urfa.

Nutritional Info: Calories: 857 | Sodium: 2551mg | Dietary Fiber: 2.9g | Total Fat: 74.1g | Total Carbs: 17.2g | Protein: 33.7g.

WHITE BEAN AND EDAMAME HUMMUS

Servings: 2-1/4 Cups | Prep Time: 20 Minutes

INGREDIENTS

1 (15-ounce) can cannellini beans

1-1/2 cups cooked edamame

2 medium garlic cloves

1/4 cup water, plus more as needed

3 tablespoons freshly squeezed lemon juice

2 tablespoons olive oil

1 teaspoon kosher salt, plus more as needed

1/4 teaspoon toasted sesame oil

Freshly ground black pepper

2 tablespoons fresh cilantro

Taro chips, for serving (optional)

This hummus has an Asian flair thanks to the edamame, and the replacement of chickpeas with white beans. It gets a light nutty flavor from the addition of sesame oil.

DIRECTIONS

1. Drain and rinse the cannellini beans. Shell the edamame, and thaw if using frozen edamame. Coarsely chop the garlic and cilantro.

2. Put all the ingredients EXCEPT for the cilantro in your food processor, and process on speed 2 until smooth. If the dip is too thick, add water, and pulse. Repeat the process until desired consistency is reached.

3. Place the mixture in a bowl, and stir in the cilantro. Add more lemon juice, and salt to taste.

4. Serve with taro chips, or chips of your choice.

Nutritional Info: Calories: 998 | Sodium: 1111mg | Dietary Fiber: 54.4g | Total Fat: 26.3g | Total Carbs: 133.1g | Protein: 66.9g.

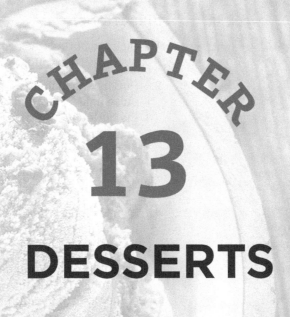

CHAPTER
13

DESSERTS

APPLE CROSTATA

Servings: 6 | Prep Time: 20 Minutes | Bake Time: 25 Minutes

INGREDIENTS

FOR THE CRUST:

1 cup all-purpose flour

2 tablespoons granulated sugar

1/4 teaspoon kosher salt

1 stick very cold unsalted butter

2 tablespoons ice water

FOR THE FILLING:

3 large apples

1/4 teaspoon grated orange zest

1/4 cup flour

1/4 cup granulated or superfine sugar

1/4 teaspoon kosher salt

1/4 teaspoon ground cinnamon

1/8 teaspoon ground allspice

1/2 stick cold unsalted butter

A crostata is an Italian pie or tart with a chunky filling. It ha a wonderful flavor similar to apple pie.

DIRECTIONS

1. Dice the butter. Peel, core, and slice the apples into 8 wedges. Then roughly slice the wedges into 3 chunks.

2. Put the sugar, flour, and salt in your food processor, and pulse until well mixed. Put in the butter and pulse until the butter becomes pea sized. Hold the pulse button, and pour in the ice water. Then continue to pulse until right before the dough is about to become a solid mass

3. Put the dough on a floured surface and shape it into a disk. Refrigerate, wrapped in plastic for an hour.

4. Mix the apple with the orange zest. Place the apples on the dough, making sure to leave a 1-1/2-inch border.

5. Put the allspice, cinnamon, sugar, flour, and salt in your Hamilton Beach food processor, and pulse a few times to combine. Put in the butter, and pulse again until the contents become crumbly.

6. Transfer to a bowl and massage with your hands until the mixture begins to hold together. Place the mixture evenly on top of the apples. Then gently fold the borders over the apples. Care pleat the dough.

7. Bake until the apples are soft, and the crust turns a golden brown, around 20 to 25 minutes. Let the crostata cool.

8. Serve the crostata warm, or at room temperature.

Nutritional Info: Calories: 404 | Sodium: 359mg | Dietary Fiber: 3.5g | Total Fat: 23.5g | Total Carbs: 48.0g | Protein: 3.2g.

APRICOT GALETTE

Servings: 6 | Prep Time: 20 Minutes | Bake Time: 30 Minutes

INGREDIENTS

1/4 cup sliced almonds

1/4 cup confectioners' sugar

6 fresh apricots

1 sheet frozen puff pastry sheets

1 tablespoon granulated sugar

A galette is a French round crusty cake. You can control how tart the galette is by choosing less or more ripe apricots. The riper the apricot, the sweeter they are.

DIRECTIONS

1. Remove the pit from the apricots, and slice them into 1/8 inch wedges. Lightly grease a shallow baking pan with butter. Preheat your oven to 425F.

2. Place the almonds and confectioners' sugar in your food processor, and pulse until they're ground finely.

3. Place the puff pastry on a lightly floured surface. Unfold the sheet, and carefully cut out a 9 inch round piece. Place the cut out circle in the baking.

4. Use a fork to poke the entire circle. Spread the almonds evenly all over the dough leaving 1/4 border all around. Place the apricots on top of the almonds, allowing the apricots to overlap, creating a decorative design. Top with powdered sugar.

5. Bake the galette for around 30 minutes, until the dough turns into a golden crust. Transfer to a wire rack to cool.

Nutritional Info: Calories: 302 | Sodium: 102mg | Dietary Fiber: 1.8g | Total Fat: 17.7g | Total Carbs: 33.3g | Protein: 4.3g.

BANANA NUTELLA ICE CREAM

Servings: 2 | Prep Time: 5 Minutes

INGREDIENTS

5 frozen bananas

1/2 teaspoon vanilla

3/4 cups Nutella

This is a dessert that you can serve your kids without guilt. It contains no dairy, and only 3 ingredients, Nutella, banana, and vanilla.

DIRECTIONS

1. Put the bananas in your food process, and process on speed 1 until completely smooth. Make sure you scrape the bits off the bowl throughout. The bananas should look like ice cream.

2. Add in the remaining ingredients and pulse until the ingredients are well mixed.

3. Serve immediately or store in the freezer in an airtight container.

Nutritional Info: Calories: 744 | Sodium: 39mg | Dietary Fiber: 12.4g | Total Fat: 27.3g | Total Carbs: 122.5g | Protein: 8.0g.

CHEESECAKE

Servings: 12 | Prep Time: 15 Minutes + 2 Hours for cooling | Bake Time: 45 Minutes

INGREDIENTS

pack graham crackers

tablespoons white sugar

/2 cup butter

-1/2 teaspoons ground cinnamon

-ounce cream cheese

cup white sugar

eggs

-1/2 teaspoons vanilla extract

6-ounce sour cream

teaspoons white sugar

teaspoon vanilla extract

This is a delicious traditional cheesecake recipe. It can be spiced up with your favorite garnish on top such as blueberries.

DIRECTIONS

1. Put the cream cheese and butter out to soften. Preheat your oven to 375 F.

2. Put the graham crackers, cinnamon, and 2 tablespoons sugar in your food processor, and pulse until the mixture is smooth. Transfer the mixture to a 8x12 baking dish, and press it in to the bottom to form the crust.

3. Put the cream cheese, eggs, vanilla, and 1 cup sugar in the food processor, and process on speed 1 until the mixture is smooth. Transfer the mixture to the baking dish, spreading it evenly over the crust.

4. Bake until the filling sets, around 25 to 30 minutes. Let the cheesecake cool for 2 hours.

5. After the cheesecake has cooled, preheat your oven to 350F. Combine the remaining sugar, sour cream, and vanilla in a bowl and mix until well combined. Cover the top of the cheesecake with the mixture. Bake for an additional 10-15 minutes.

6. Allow the cheesecake to cool before serving.

Nutritional Info: Calories: 450 | Sodium: 273mg | Dietary Fiber: 0.0g | Total Fat: 36.7g | Total Carbs: 25.1g | Protein: 7.1g.

CHOCOLATE HAZELNUT BISCOTTI

Servings: 30 Biscotti | Prep Time: 40 Minutes | Bake Time: 70 Minutes

INGREDIENTS

1 cup hazelnuts

4 ounces semisweet chocolate

1 cup firmly packed light brown sugar

1-3/4 cups all-purpose flour

1/3 cup unsweetened cocoa powder

1 tablespoon instant espresso powder

1 teaspoon baking soda

1/4 teaspoon salt

3 large eggs

1-1/2 teaspoons pure vanilla extract

Biscotti are Italian biscuit cookies. They're traditionally served with coffee, and used for dipping. These biscotti have a deep chocolate flavor with a nice nuttiness from the hazelnuts.

Nutritional Info: Calories: 91 | Sodium: 72mg | Dietary Fiber: 0.9g | Total Fat: 3.3g | Total Carbs: 13.6g | Protein: 2.2g.

DIRECTIONS

1. Coarsely chop the chocolate. Preheat your oven to 350 F.

2. Put the hazelnuts on a baking sheet, and toast in the oven for around 15 minutes. The hazelnuts will start to brown, blister, and become fragrant when ready.

3. Once toasted, cover the hazelnuts with a towel, and allow them to steam for 5 minutes. Then remove the skin from the hazelnut using the towel. Let the hazelnuts cool completely, and then chop them coarsely.

4. Lower your oven to 300F. Use parchment paper to line a big baking sheet.

5. Place the chocolate and brown sugar in your food processor, and process on speed 1 until the chocolate is finely ground.

6. Whisk together the espresso, cocoa powder, baking soda, salt, and flour.

7. Use an electric mixer or hand mixer to beat the eggs, and vanilla extract until thoroughly mixed. Add in the other 2 mixtures and continue to mix the mixtures. Halfway through the mixtures combining add in the hazelnuts, and continue to mix until a dough is formed. The dough should be stiff.

8. Flour your hands and separate the dough into 2 equals portions. Place the dough on a lightly floured surface, and roll it into 2 logs that are about 2 inches wide, and 10 inches long.

9. Put the logs on the lined baking sheet. Make sure they are at least 3 inches apart. Bake them for 35 to 40 minutes, until the logs are just about firm, but not quite firm. Allow the logs to cool for 10 minutes on a wire rack.

10. Place the logs on a cutting board using a long spatula if you have one. Slice the logs into 3/4-inch thick pieces on a diagonal using a serrated knife.

11. Put the pieces cut side down back onto the baking sheet. Bake for 15 minutes, and then flip the pieces, and bake for around another 15 minutes. The biscotti should by dry, and crispy when they're done. Allow the biscotti to cool on a wire rack before serving.

12. Serve the biscotti at room temperature.

CHOCOLATE ICE CREAM

Servings: 6-8 | Prep Time: 5 Hours 35 Minutes | Cook Time: 5 Minutes

INGREDIENTS

3/4 cups cocoa powder

1 cup sugar

3 cups milk

1 cup water

This ice cream has only 4 ingredients, but it tastes fantastic. Using a high quality cocoa powder is essential to getting the best chocolate flavor.

DIRECTIONS

1. Whisk the sugar, cocoa, and 1/2 cup water in a small sauce pan on medium heat until it turns into a paste. Put in the rest of the water, and let cook, stirring frequently for around 5 minutes until the sugar dissolves, and the mixture is warm.

2. Take the saucepan off heat and put in the milk.

3. Place the mixture in a metal 13X9 baking pan, and place it in the freezer for at least 5 hours, until the mixture is frozen.

4. Once frozen, put half of the frozen mixture in your food process, and process on speed 1 until the mixture reaches the texture of ice cream. Repeat the process with the other half of the mixture.

5. Put the ice cream in a freezer safe container, and freeze for 30 minutes.

6. Serve after the 30 Minutes.

Nutritional Info: Calories: 157 | Sodium: 46mg | Dietary Fiber: 2.4g | Total Fat: 2.9g | Total Carbs: 33.9g | Protein: 4.5g.

CHOCOLATE MOUSSE

Servings: 6 | Prep Time: 25 Minutes | Cook Time: 5 Minutes

INGREDIENTS

ounces semisweet chocolate, coarsely
hopped

tablespoons vegetable oil

tablespoon red wine or liqueur

tablespoon pure vanilla extract

/3 cup milk or water

2 tablespoons sugar

Pinch of kosher or sea salt

cup heavy cream

Freshly ground black pepper (optional)

This mouse has a lovely velvety texture. The flavor is rich
and delicious. It pairs great with a nice red wine. Use milk in
instead of water if you want a creamier texture and flavor.

DIRECTIONS

1. Place the chocolate in your food processor and process
    on speed 1 until it's finely minced.

2. In a small bowl mix the oil, vanilla, and wine.

3. Place the sugar, milk or water, and salt in a small
    saucepan, and bring the ingredients to a simmer.
    Stir until the sugar dissolves. The moment the sugar
    dissolves, place the mixture in your food processor with
    it already turned on to speed 1.

4. Process until the chocolate melts into the mixture,
    around 15 to 20 seconds. Then add in the oil and wine
    mixture and process until well combined, around 10
    seconds. Transfer the mixture to a bowl, and allow it to
    cool.

5. Once the mixture is totally cool, beat the cream for a
    short time. It should be able to hold a soft shape. Then
    fold 1/3 of the cream into mixture. Then do the same
    with the rest of the cream until it's blended. Don't over
    fold it in.

6. Serve immediately or refrigerate until ready to serve.

Nutritional Info: Calories: 316 | Sodium: 40mg | Dietary Fiber: 1.1g | Total Fat: 22.0g | Total Carbs: 25.2g | Protein: 3.4g.

COCONUT CREAM PIE

Servings: 8 | Prep Time: 3 Hours 50 Minutes | Bake Time: 30 Minutes

INGREDIENTS

CRUST:

1-1/2 cups all-purpose flour

1 tablespoon sugar

1/2 teaspoon salt

6 tablespoons chilled unsalted butter

3 tablespoons chilled solid vegetable shortening

4 tablespoons ice water

1-1/2 cups all-purpose flour

FILLING:

1/2 cup sugar

2 large eggs

1 large egg yolk

3 tablespoons all-purpose flour

1-1/2 cups whole milk

1-1/2 cups sweetened flaked coconut

1 teaspoon vanilla extract

1/8 teaspoon coconut extract

TOPPING:

2/3 cups sweetened flaked coconut

1-1/4 cups chilled whipping cream

2 tablespoons sugar

1/8 teaspoon coconut extract

This pie is so light and filled with coconut goodness. The toasted coconut topping gives a nice crunch and contrast of texture.

Nutritional Info: Calories: 549 | Sodium: 257mg | Dietary Fiber: 3.3g | Total Fat: 30.3g | Total Carbs: 61.2g | Protein: 9.8g.

DIRECTIONS

1. Cut the vegetable shortening, and butter into 1/4-inch cubes.

2. Place the sugar, salt, and flour in your food processor and pulse until well combined. Put in the shortening and butter, and pulse the mixture until it becomes a coarse meal. Pour in the 4 tablespoons water and pulse until the mixture forms moist chunks.

3. If the mixture is too dry add cold water 1 teaspoon at a time and pulse until the moist chunks form.

4. Take the dough out of the food processor and shape it into a ball, then flatten it into a disk. Wrap the dough in plastic wrap, and refrigerate for an hour.

5. Place the dough between 2 pieces of plastic wrap, and use a rolling pin to roll it out into a 14-inch circle. Place the dough in a 9-inch glass pie dish.

6. Fold the overhanging crust underneath, and crimp edges. Use a fork to poke the bottom of the crust all over. Freeze the dough for 15 minutes.

7. Preheat your oven to 375F while freezing.

8. Line the frozen crust with aluminum foil. Use dried beans to fill the pie crust. Bake for 20 minutes, and then remove the foil and beans.

9. Put the crust bake in the oven, and bake for around 10 minutes, until the crust turns golden. Allow the crust to cool.

10. Use a whisk to mix together the egg yolks, flour, eggs, and 1/2 cup sugar for the filling.

11. In a medium sauce pan, place the milk and coconut, and bring the mixture to a simmer on medium heat.

12. Slowly whisk the hot mixture into the egg/flour mixture. Place the mixture back in the sauce pan, and cook for around 4 minutes, until the mixture thickens and boils, make sure to stir frequently throughout.

13. Take the mixture off the heat, and stir in the vanilla and coconut extract. Put the mixture in a bowl, and put plastic wrap directly on the mixture.

14. Place it in the refrigerator for at least 2 hours, until the mixture is cold. Place the cold filling in the pie crust and refrigerate overnight.

15. Put the coconut for the topping in a skillet, and toast on medium heat for about 3 minutes, until the coconut is lightly browned. Once brown, allow the coconut to cool.

16. Put the sugar, coconut extract, and cream in a bowl and beat it using an electric mixer until the mixture forms peaks. Spread over the top of the pie, and garnish with the toasted coconut.

17. Serve the pie cold.

CRANBERRY SPICE CAKE

Servings: 8 | Prep Time: 20 Minutes | Bake Time: 1 Hour 10 Minutes

INGREDIENTS

CAKE:

Nonstick vegetable oil spray

1-1/2 cups all-purpose flour

3/4 teaspoons ground cinnamon

3/4 teaspoons kosher salt

1/2 teaspoon ground cardamom

1 teaspoon baking powder

1/2 teaspoon baking soda

2 cups frozen cranberries

2/3 cups sugar

2/3 cups dark brown sugar

1/2 cup grapeseed oil

2 large eggs

1/2 cup sour cream

1 tablespoon fresh orange zest

2 teaspoons fresh lemon zest

1 teaspoon vanilla extract

1/2 cup apple cider

LEMON GLAZE:

1 cup powdered sugar

2 teaspoons fresh lemon zest

3 tablespoons fresh lemon juice

1/8 teaspoon kosher salt

This cake taste like a cranberry muffin, and gingerbread had a child. It's a perfect dessert for holiday time.

Nutritional Info: Calories: 449 | Sodium: 363mg | Dietary Fiber: 2.0g | Total Fat: 18.2g | Total Carbs: 67.5g | Protein: 4.6g.

DIRECTIONS

1. If using frozen cranberries, thaw them out. Strain the lemon juice. Preheat your oven to 350F. Grease the sides, and bottom of a cake pan with the cooking spray. Use parchment paper to line the bottom of the cake pan.

2. Use a whisk to combine the cinnamon, flour, cardamom, salt, baking soda, and baking powder.

3. Put the cranberries in your food processor, and pulse until the cranberries are finely chopped.

4. Mix the oil, brown sugar, and sugar together. Mix in the eggs 1 at a time. Then use a whisk in the lemon zest, vanilla, sour cream, and orange zest.

5. Whisk the flour mixture into the oil and sugar mixture in 3 batches. Whisk in the apple cider in 2-1/4 cups batches in between the flour batches. Once combined, fold the cranberries into the mixture. Transfer the mixture to the cake pan, and smooth out the top.

6. Bake the cake for about 1 hour 10 minutes, rotating the cake halfway through the baking process. The cake is ready when a toothpick can go into the center of the cake, and come out clean. Cool the cake for 15 minutes on a wire rack. Use a knife to cut around the edges of the cake. Remove the cake from the pan. Remove the parchment paper, and invert the cake. Allow the cake to cool for another 20 minutes.

7. While the cake is baking, whisk together the lemon juice, salt, powdered sugar, and lemon zest together for glaze. Cover the top of the warm cake with the glaze, and let the glaze fall down the sides of the cake.

8. Let the glazed cake rest for at least an hour before serving.

CREAM CHEESE PIE CRUST

Servings: 2 | Prep Time: 1 Hour 15 Minutes

INGREDIENTS

2 cups plus 4 tablespoons all-purpose flour

2 tablespoons white sugar

1/2 teaspoon salt

1-1/2 sticks cold unsalted butter

6 ounces cold cream cheese

3 tablespoons cold heavy whipping cream

This pie crust is incredibly flakey, and tender thanks to the cream cheese. This recipe makes 2 crusts, or a top and bottom for one pie. Fill it with your favorite pie filling.

DIRECTIONS

1. Cut the cream cheese, and butter into 1/4-inch cubes.

2. Whisk the sugar, salt, and flour together until well combined.

3. Place all of the ingredients in your food processor, starting with the dry ingredients, and pulse until the mixture becomes crumbly with pea sized pieces of butter and cream cheese.

4. Transfer the mixture to a bowl, and drizzle the cream over the mixture. Use a spatula to mix, until the mixture becomes moist chunks.

5. Create 2 equal size pieces out of the dough, and form them into disks. Refrigerate for at least 1 hour. Place the dough in a pie tin, fill it with your favorite dough, and bake.

Nutritional Info: Calories: 368 | Sodium: 335mg | Dietary Fiber: 0.8g | Total Fat: 26.6g | Total Carbs: 27.6g | Protein: 5.1g.

LEMON CURD

INGREDIENTS

1/2 cup butter

Zest from 3 large lemons

1-1/2 cups sugar

5 large eggs

1/2 cup fresh lemon Juice

Lemon curd is incredibly versatile, and its uses are endless. Try using it as a filling for cakes, a spread for toast, or a topper for shortbread cookies.

DIRECTIONS

1. Put the butter out to soften.

2. Put the sugar, zest, and butter in your food processor, and pulse until mixed together. One by one add in the eggs and lemon juice, process on speed 1 until the mixture is smooth.

3. Transfer mixture to a sauce pan, and heat on low heat. Stir constantly throughout. Use a cooking or candy thermometer to keep track of the curd's temperature. Take curd off the heat when it reaches 170F.

4. Allow to cool before transferring to an airtight container, and refrigerating.

Nutritional Info: Calories: 205 | Sodium: 40mg | Dietary Fiber: 0.0g | Total Fat: 4.5g | Total Carbs: 42.7g | Protein: 1.3g.

PEACH BLACKBERRY TART

Servings: 8-10 | Prep Time: 1 Hour | Bake Time: 1 Hour 10 Minutes

INGREDIENTS

FOR THE CRUST:

1/3 cup whole or sliced almonds

1 cup all-purpose flour

3 tablespoons sugar

1/4 teaspoon salt

8 tablespoons cold butter

2 tablespoons ice cold water

FOR THE GLAZE:

1 peach

Zest of 1 small Meyer lemon

Juice from lemon

2/3 cups sugar

1/2 cup water

FOR THE FILLING AND TOPPING:

8 ounces softened cream cheese

8 ounces softened mascarpone

1/3 cup confectioners' sugar

3/4 cups fresh blackberries

1 tablespoon vanilla extract

1/4 teaspoon almond extract

1/8 teaspoon cinnamon

Shave of fresh nutmeg

3 large or 4 medium firm peaches

1/4 cup almonds or macadamia nuts

This tart is perfect for summertime when peaches, and blackberries are at the peak of freshness. It makes a beautiful dessert with a delicious almond flavored crust.

Nutritional Info: Calories: 404 | Sodium: 211mg | Dietary Fiber: 2.4g | Total Fat: 24.5g | Total Carbs: 41.7g | Protein: 7.2g.

DIRECTIONS

1. Dice the peach for the glaze. Slice the peaches for the topping into thin slices. Cut the butter into small pieces. Set the mascarpone and cream cheese out to soften. Mash 1/4 cup of the blackberries. Preheat your oven to 375F.

2. In a shallow saucepan, toast 1/3 cup of almonds on medium-low heat. Toss the almonds often while toasting. Toast until the almonds turn golden. Once toasted, place the almonds in a bowl, and allow them to cool.

3. Once the almonds have cooled, place them along with the sugar, salt, and flour in your food processor. Pulse the mixture until it's finely ground. Put in the butter, and pulse again until a coarse meal is formed. Then put in 2 tablespoons of water, and pulse again until a dough starts to form.

4. Transfer the dough to a piece of plastic wrap, and shape it into a disk. Place it in the refrigerator, wrapped tightly for 15 to 20 minutes.

5. Push the chilled dough into the sides and bottom of a 10-inch tart pan, ideally with a removable bottom.

6. Cover the pan with plastic wrap and place in the freezer for 15 minutes.

7. Use parchment paper to line the tart pan, and fill the tart pan with dried beans. Put the pan on a baking sheet, and bake for about 15 to 20 minutes, until the sides start to turn brown.

8. Discard the beans and parchment paper, and let the crust cook for around 20 more minutes, until the crust turns a nice golden brown.

9. Place the lemon juice, lemon zest, water, sugar, and diced peach in a small saucepan, and bring to a simmer on medium heat. Cook for 20 to 30 minutes, until the mixture thickens.

10. Once thickened, strain the glaze; and throw out the solid pieces. Set aside the glaze for later.

11. Mix together the mashed blackberries, confectioners' sugar, mascarpone and cream cheese, nutmeg, cinnamon, and vanilla and almond extract until they become a smooth mixture.

12. Transfer the mixture to the crust.

13. Place the sliced peaches on top of the filing in a circular pattern. Mix the rest of the berries, and nuts with the glaze, and carefully top the tart with it. Don't use all of it.

14. Brush the peaches with more of the glaze. Serve immediately, and serve with leftover glaze.

PISTACHIO CAKE

Servings: 8 | Prep Time: 20 Minutes | Bake Time: 30 to 40 Minutes

INGREDIENTS

3/4 cups unsalted pistachios (approximately
4 ounces; not dyed red)

1 cup all-purpose flour

2 teaspoons baking powder

1 teaspoon ground cardamom

1/4 teaspoon salt

1/2 cup whole milk

1/4 teaspoon pure vanilla extract

1/2 cup (1 stick) unsalted butter

1 cup sugar

3 large eggs

2 tablespoons finely grated orange zest
(from 3 medium oranges)

This wonderful cake combines the nuttiness of pistachios, and the aromatic citrus flavor of orange zest. The cake is very moist, and is perfect for dessert, or with coffee and tea.

Nutritional Info: Calories: 338 | Sodium: 220mg | Dietary Fiber: 3.0g | Total Fat: 16.7g | Total Carbs: 44.5g | Protein: 6.0g.

DIRECTIONS

1. Set the butter out to soften. Shell the pistachios. Place a rack in the middle of your oven. Preheat your oven to 350F. Grease a 9 inch round baking pan with butter, and use wax paper to line the bottom of it. Use the butter to lightly grease the wax paper as well. Use flour to dust the pan. Get rid of any excess flour.

2. Place the pistachios in your food processor, and pulse them until they're ground up finely. Make sure you do not over process, or the pistachios will become a paste. Put in the salt, flour, cardamom, and baking powder, and pulse for a short time until the ingredients are combined.

3. Mix the vanilla and milk in a bowl.

4. Beat the butter and sugar using an electric mixer on medium speed, until the mixture is fluffy. Then beat in the eggs one at a time, until well mixed.

5. Lower the speed to low, and mix in a batch of the pistachios, then a batch of the vanilla milk. Keeping on alternating between the 2 mixtures until they're both mixed in. Make sure you start and end with the pistachio mixture. Then beat in the orange zest.

6. Pour the mixture into the baking pan, making sure to distribute evenly. Bake for 30 to 40 minutes, until a toothpick can be stuck in the middle of the cake, and come out clean.

7. Allow the cake to cool in the pan for 10 minutes. After the 10 minutes use a knife to loosen the cake by running it around the entire edge of the cake. Carefully invert the cake on a rack. Discard the paper.

8. Serve the cake warm. Top with whip cream, or serve witch ice cream if desired.

SKILLET CHOCOLATE CHIP COOKIE

Servings: 10-12 | Prep Time: 10 Minutes | Bake Time: 15-20 Minutes

INGREDIENTS

1/2 cup butter, at room temperature

1/2 cup packed brown sugar

1/4 cup sugar

1 large egg

1 teaspoon vanilla extract

1-1/2 cups all-purpose flour

1 teaspoon. baking soda

1/2 teaspoon salt

1 – 1-1/2 cups chocolate chips

1/2 cup pecans or walnuts (optional)

Now you can make this favorite dessert at home instead ordering it at a restaurant. It makes a delicious dense cookie pizza and is so quick to make.

DIRECTIONS

1. Make sure the butter is at room temperature, and not cold. Chop the pecans or walnuts if using them. Preheat your oven to 350F.

2. Place the butter and brown sugar in your food processor, and pulse and their well combined. Put in the vanilla and egg, and process on speed 1 until the ingredients turn a pale color, and the mixture becomes creamy. Scrape the sides if necessary.

3. Put in the salt, baking soda, and flour in and pulse until a dough is almost formed. Put in the chocolate chips, and nuts if desired, and pulse until dough is formed.

4. Transfer the dough to a large cast iron skillet, and press it down into the skillet making sure it's packed into the bottom and sides. Bake until the cookie turns a pale golden color, and the cookie sets, 15 to 20 minutes.

5. Slice and serve.

Nutritional Info: Calories: 283 | Sodium: 280mg | Dietary Fiber: 1.1g | Total Fat: 14.5g | Total Carbs: 34.6g | Protein: 3.8g.

VANILLA CRUMB CAKE

Servings: 8-10 | Prep Time: 15 Minutes | Bake Time: 40-45 Minutes

INGREDIENTS

cup + 2 tablespoons sugar

2/3 cups cold butter

2-1/4 cups all-purpose flour

1/2 teaspoon salt

1-1/2 teaspoons vanilla extract

1/2 teaspoon baking soda

1/2 teaspoon baking powder

2 large eggs

1/2 cup buttermilk

This a delicious coffee cake that's easy to make. It's truly for vanilla lovers, because it replaces the typical spiced flavors of crumb cake with vanilla.

DIRECTIONS

1. Cut the butter into chunks. Preheat your oven to 350F. Use butter or cooking spray to grease a deep 9-inch pie place lightly.

2. Put the butter, salt, flour, vanilla extract, and sugar in your food processor and pulse until the butter is well mixed in and the mixture turns sandy.

3. Take out 1-1/2 cups of the mixture and place it on a cutting board. Use your hands to form chunky crumbs out of the mixture. When it forms a good crumb, place the mixture in the refrigerator for a few minutes.

4. While the crumb is in the refrigerator, put the baking powder and baking soda in your food processor with the remaining mixture.

5. Pulse the mixture until the new ingredients are well incorporated. Put in the milk and eggs, and process on speed 1 until a batter is formed. Scrape down the sides if necessary and pulse until those bits are incorporated.

6. Transfer the batter to the lightly greased pie pan. Distribute the crumb topping evenly on top of the batter. Bake the cake until you a place a toothpick in the middle of the cake and it comes out clean, around 40 to 45 minutes.

7. Allow the cake to cool to room temperature before slicing.

8. Serve at room temperature.

Nutritional Info: Calories: 307 | Sodium: 294mg | Dietary Fiber: 0.8g | Total Fat: 13.6g | Total Carbs: 42.4g | Protein: 4.7g.

COCONUT SHORTBREAD LEMONGRASS BARS

Servings: 8-12 | Prep Time: 35 Minutes | Bake Time: 50 Minutes

INGREDIENTS

FOR THE CRUST:

1-1/2 cups all-purpose flour

1 cup unsweetened shredded coconut

1/2 cup powdered sugar

1/2 teaspoon salt

1/2 cup plus three tablespoons unsalted butter

FOR THE FILLING

1-1/4 cups sugar

3 lemongrass stalks

5 tablespoons lemon juice

3 large eggs

1/4 cup flour

1/4 cup powdered sugar

These bars are packed with so much flavor. The tartness o the lemongrass balances out the sweetness of the sugar, and the shortbread gives these bars a nice buttery flavor.

DIRECTIONS

1. Make sure the butter is at room temperature. Finely chop the lemongrass. Preheat your oven to 350F. Grease a 13x9x2 baking pan with butter.

2. Beat the powdered sugar, coconut, salt, and flour until well mixed using an electric mixer. Turn the mixer to low, and put in the butter, mix the ingredients until ther are moist chunks. Then place the dough in the greased pan, and press it up the sides about 1/2-inch, and into the bottom of the pan.

3. Place the crust in the oven, and bake around 25 minutes, until the crust becomes golden.

4. Lower the oven temperature to 325F.

5. Pulse the sugar, and lemongrass in your food processo until the lemongrass is ground up. This should take around 1 minutes.

6. Put in the lemon juice and process on speed 1 until well mixed. Then put in the egg, and process on speed 1 until well mixed. Put in a pinch of salt, and flour, and pulse until mixture becomes smooth.

7. Distribute the mixture evenly on top of the crust and bake for around 25 minutes. The filling should be firm. Allow the bars to cool on a rack while still in the pan.

8. After the bars have cooled, garnish with powdered sugar, and serve.

Nutritional Info: Calories: 530 | Sodium: 173mg | Dietary Fiber: 2.2g | Total Fat: 11.8g | Total Carbs: 100.4g | Protein: 8.1g.

WATERMELON GRANITA WITH BLUEBERRIES

Servings: 6 | Prep Time: 2 to 4 hours

INGREDIENTS

6 cups (about 2 pounds) seedless watermelon

1/2 cup fresh lime juice

1/3 cup agave nectar

2 cups fresh blueberries

6 mint sprigs (optional)

Granita is similar to a snow cone, but with real fruit. This dish is the perfect dessert for summer with the combination of watermelon, blueberry, and lime.

DIRECTIONS

1. Cut the watermelon into cubes.

2. Place the watermelon in batches in your food processor, and puree on speed 2. Use a sieve to strain the puree, and throw out the solid parts. Place the watermelon liquid, agave, and lime juice in metal 9x11 pan, and place it in the freezer.

3. Use a fork to scrape the mixture every 20 to 30 minutes. Continue to do this until mixture resembles small crystals. This should take between 2 and 4 hours. Once the granite is done freezing, scrape it once more and then divide it into 6 portions.

4. Top the granite with blueberries, and mint springs, and serve immediately.

Nutritional Info: Calories: 307 | Sodium: 294mg | Dietary Fiber: 0.8g | Total Fat: 13.6g | Total Carbs: 42.4g | Protein: 4.7g.

CHAPTER
14
PANTRY

ITEMS TO KEEP ON HAND

It's a good idea to have certain items on hand that are used often in cooking. A high-quality salt is a must. Avoid table salt and instead go for a natural salt like sea salt, or rock salt. These natural salts are free of chemicals, and provide more nutrients. Your favorite vegetables, especially organic ones, for soups, purees, and salads. Always keep broth/stock on hand. Broth/stock is used in many soups, and can be used in place of water to cook grains for added flavor. All-purpose flour is a necessity if you plan on baking. It's also used to thicken soups and other dishes. Look for organic flour that hasn't been bleached. Eggs are always good to have on hand, especially for desserts and baking. Milk is good to have on hand for both baking and soups. Many baking recipes call for milk, and it can also be used to make soups creamier. Lastly always have some form of semi-sweet-chocolate on hand. Chocolate is used in many desserts, as well as Mexican cuisine. You can use it to garnish your desserts too. It also comes in handy when you want to satisfy your sweet tooth.

KITCHEN UNIT CONVERSION

1 teaspoon = 1/3 tbsp =	4.9 ml
1 dessertspoon = 2 tsp =	9.9 ml
1 tablespoon = 1.5 dstsp / 3 tsp =	14.8 ml
1 fuid ounce = 2 tbsp / 6 tsp =	29.6 ml
1 cup = 16 tbsp / 48 tsp =	236.6 ml
1 quart = 4 cup =	946 ml
1 gal = 4 quart / 16 cup =	3.79 l
1 ounce = 2 tbsp =	28.4 g
1 pounds = 16 oz =	453.6 g

Made in the USA
Monee, IL
29 November 2024

71623899R00090